Towards a Cross-Linguistic Assessment
of Speech Production

Kasseler Arbeiten
zur Sprache und Literatur
Anglistik-Germanistik-Romanistik

Herausgegeben von
Horst Grünert, Manfred Raupach,
Martin Schulze

Band 7

Verlag Peter D. Lang
Frankfurt a.M • Bern • Cirencester/U.K.

Hans W. Dechert/
Manfred Raupach (eds.)

Towards a Cross-Linguistic Assessment of Speech Production

Verlag Peter D. Lang
Frankfurt a.M. • Bern • Cirencester/U.K.

CIP-Kurztitelaufnahme der Deutschen Bibliothek

Towards a cross-linguistic assessment of speech production / Hans W. Dechert ; Manfred Raupach (eds.). - Frankfurt a.M., Bern, Cirencester/U.K. : Lang, 1980.
 (Kasseler Arbeiten zur Sprache und Literatur ; Bd. 7)
 ISBN 3-8204-6003-9

NE: Dechert, Hans-Wilhelm [Hrsg.]

ISBN 3-8204-6003-9
© Verlag Peter D. Lang GmbH, Frankfurt am Main 1980
Alle Rechte vorbehalten.
Nachdruck oder Vervielfältigung, auch auszugsweise, in allen Formen wie Mikrofilm, Xerographie, Mikrofiche, Mikrocard, Offset verboten.
Druck: fotokop Wilhelm Weihert KG, Darmstadt
Umschlaggestaltung: Stefan Platen, Marktplatz 5, 6360 Friedberg

CONTENTS

PREFACE

CROSS–LINGUISTIC DESCRIPTIONS OF SPEECH
PERFORMANCE AS A CONTRIBUTION TO
'CONTRASTIVE PSYCHOLINGUISTICS'
Manfred Raupach 9

CROSS–LINGUISTIC INVESTIGATION OF SOME
TEMPORAL DIMENSIONS OF SPEECH
Daniel C. O'Connell 23

TEMPORAL VARIABLES WITHIN AND
BETWEEN LANGUAGES
François Grosjean 39

THE ANALYSIS OF CROSS–LANGUAGE COMMUNICATION:
PROLEGOMENA TO THE THEORY AND METHODOLOGY
Kari Sajavaara and Jaakko Lehtonen 55

REPETITION AND CORRECTION AS AN INDICATION
OF SPEECH PLANNING AND EXECUTION PROCESSES
AMONG SECOND LANGUAGE LEARNERS
Ann K. Fathman 77

UTTERANCE PLANNING AND CORRECTION BEHAVIOR:
ITS FUNCTION IN THE GRAMMAR CONSTRUCTION
PROCESS FOR SECOND LANGUAGE LEARNERS
Herbert W. Seliger 87

CONTEXTUAL HYPOTHESIS–TESTING–PROCEDURES
IN SPEECH PRODUCTION
Hans W. Dechert 101

TEMPORAL VARIABLES IN CROSS–LINGUISTIC
PSYCHOLINGUISTICS
– AN ANNOTATED BIBLIOGRAPHY
Richard Wiese 123

PREFACE

This collection is the result of endeavours by the Kassel Psycho- and Pragmalinguistic Research Group (KAPPA) to establish contacts and an exchange of ideas with other researchers working on the psycholinguistic assessment of speech production. It comprises articles written by different researchers having different linguistic backgrounds and dealing with different languages. In this sense it tries for the first time to give an overview of various methodological attempts to compare speech data from a cross-linguistic point of view. Thus the following contributions deal with the comparison of speech data taken from
- native speakers of different languages, or
- native speakers and language learners of the same language, or
- speakers in their native and their second languages.

Since we have been particularly interested in the analysis of learner speech, it is this problem of second language performance that is the central topic, besides more basic methodological considerations. There can be no doubt that the articles collected in this book cover only a small scope of possible models of speech production and cross-linguistic comparisons. Certainly more work needs to be done.

We believe, however, that studies of this type open the view to a new area of psycholinguistic research which has previously remained largely unexplored. The purpose of the review of the literature in the final chapter is to outline this historical dimension.

We are inclined to call this area of research "Contrastive Psycholinguistics", because we believe that Contrastive Analysis and Error Analysis, despite certain merits in predicting, analysing, and describing "errors" in second language production, actually offer little aid in a psycholinguistic understanding of the planning and execution of second language performance.

Whether we and our co-authors are right in our attempt to delineate this new area must be shown by further discussion and research. At present it is our hope that this collection of articles dealing with various aspects of cross-linguistic comparison may inspire such a discussion.

Kassel, Germany   August 1979

H. W. D. and M. R.

CROSS-LINGUISTIC DESCRIPTIONS OF SPEECH PERFORMANCE AS A CONTRIBUTION TO 'CONTRASTIVE PSYCHOLINGUISTICS'

Manfred Raupach
University of Kassel

According to Clark and Clark (1977 : 4), the psychology of language is fundamentally concerned with the following broad questions:

(1) By what mental processes do people listen to, comprehend, and remember what they hear? *Comprehension*

(2) By what mental processes do people come to say what they say? *Production*

(3) What course do children follow in learning to comprehend and produce their first language, and why? *Acquisition*

In keeping with these questions, ‚contrastive psycholinguistics' which explicitly introduces into this field of research the additional notion of comparison, should concentrate on:

— the mental processes underlying language comprehension, production, and acquisition of people belonging to different language groups;
— the mental processes underlying language comprehension, production, and acquisition of learners of second languages in comparison
  — with the mental processes of native speakers of the target language or
  — with the mental processes of the same learners in their own native language;
— the mental processes underlying language comprehension, production, and acquisition of bilinguals.

In pursuit of the main subject of the present volume, we would like to discuss, in such a contrastive perspective, only one of these topics: the psycholinguistic significance of cross-linguistic descriptions of speech production. With reference to one of the objectives of the Kassel Research Group (KAPPA), we shall primarily deal with those studies that confront first and second language speech performance and deliberately omit problems of bilingualism.

The psycholinguistic significance of cross-linguistic descriptions of speech performance is not at all obvious in comparison, for example, with studies of interlingual word associations (Russell and Meseck, 1959; Rosenzweig, 1961; Kolers,

1963; Miron and Wolfe, 1964 and others). It is true that, in recent years, in keeping with a growing interest in the information processing aspects of linguistic performance, analyses of unpremeditated or semi-prepared utterances of speakers in their native languages have provided valuable hypotheses for speech production models (cf. Dechert and Raupach, forthcoming); but it is difficult to imagine what additional insights into the mental processes and capacities underlying human ability to use language might be obtained from comparisons of speech performance in different languages.

Three types of comparison are of particular interest for our discussion:

(1) Comparisons of speech performance of native speakers of different languages; they might supply information relating to universal vs. language specific factors in speech performance

(2) Comparisons of speech performance of native speakers and learners of that language; they might reveal forms of verbal behavior that belong specifically to learners of a second language

(3) Comparisons of first and second language speech performance of the same speaker; they might reveal forms of verbal behavior characteristic of individual second language learners.

1. *Universal vs. Language Specific Factors*

It is the first type of comparison, more than others, that has attracted the attention of psycholinguists. Cross-linguistic descriptions of this type are usually based on an analysis of 'temporal variables', such as the speaking/articulation rate or the duration and distribution of pauses. Sometimes the so-called hesitation phenomena, such as filled pauses, repeats, drawls, etc. are also taken into account. In contrast to this, speech errors, such as slips of the tongue, or intonation contours have been of minor interest up until now.

As stated above, these cross-linguistic descriptions aim primarily at a distinction between universal aspects of temporal organization and language specific characteristics. Some findings of Grosjean, who extended his comparisons to include sign languages, can serve to illustrate the direction of such research. Grosjean (forthcoming) postulates that

> all languages (oral or visual) will be characterized by the same rate of information output if such aspects as age of speaker, linguistic task, situation etc. are controlled.

But there are, in addition, language specific differences that Grosjean noted in his comparison of utterances of French and English speakers:

> We can postulate from this that spoken utterances in different oral languages will probably have identical pause time ratio (...) but that each lan-

guage will distribute the pause time in such a way that it reflects the linguistic structure of the language.

Results of this kind suggest some remarks concerning their psycholinguistic significance. The analysis of temporal variables allows, in fact, general statements referring to temporal patterns of speech performance and may thus bring into question, for example, the subjective impression that some languages are spoken with more 'speed' or 'fluency' than others and that those languages thereby convey more information within the same span of time. Findings of this nature could hardly result in new models of speech performance that differ basically from those being derived from analyses of performance in one language only (Fromkin, 1971, 1973; Garrett, 1975). But there is strong evidence for accepting temporal variables as reliable indicators for the segmentation of the stream of utterance into units that underly the process of verbal planning. Hence, the findings of Grosjean and others lead to the assumption that speakers usually plan their speech according to the specific linguistic structure of their native language. The results of our first type of comparison are relevant in this connection for the rating of second language speech performance.

It appears to us, however, that these results are not always convincing. We will not dwell here on the serious problem of lack of comparability among many of the existing studies (cf. in detail O'Connell in this volume); it is even more important that there is no generally accepted idea of the function and psycholinguistic significance of temporal variables. This inconsistency, which is not restricted to cross-linguistic studies, becomes obvious if one reviews recent discussion concerning the function of the unfilled pause, one of the favorite temporal variables analyzed up until now (cf. the bibliography of Appel, Dechert, and Raupach, 1980). To give an example, we quote from Cairns and Cairns (1976 : 146), who base their conclusions on Martin (1971) and Clark (1971):

> It seems reasonable to hypothesize that the conventional pauses (those between constituents) mark points of syntactic planning by the speaker or perhaps a deliberate attempt to punctuate a difficult sentence for the hearer. At any rate conventional pauses demarcate abstract, linguistically defined segments of surface structure. Idiosyncratic pauses, on the other hand, are assumed to reflect word-finding difficulty on the part of the speaker, which is of no decoding value for the hearer and of no deep psycholinguistic significance.

The final statement to the effect that idiosyncratic pauses are of no psycholinguistic significance seems to be simply a consequence of the method chosen for analyzing the material, in view of the fact that only those phenomena that occur with some frequency at places that are defined beforehand (= conventional pauses) can be described statistically and are, thus, comparable with each other. In contrast to this approach, it might be argued — and this corresponds much more to our own position — that non-conventional pauses, which are not finding some data from our own studies, conducted within the framework of the proposed comparison of L1 and L2 speech performance. French learners of German showed in their L2 descriptions of a cartoon a strong tendency to transfer some of their native-language habits of using temporal variables. This was true, for example, for the location of unfilled pauses and especially for the frequent occurrence of syllabic prolongation (drawls), a phenomenon which seems to be characteristic of native speakers of French. The temporal patterns of the resulting L2 productions contrasted remarkably with the patterning of German speakers in their L1 descriptions of the same cartoon (Raupach, forthcoming). We do not intend to go into detail at this point, but prefer, instead, to turn to other categories and to other levels that are relevant to cross-linguistic descriptions.

We shall illustrate our suggestions by referring for the most part to results from one of our experiments carried out, for various reasons, in the tradition of F. Bartlett. It also provided some clues regarding planning processes specific to learners of a second language. Native speakers of French (7 Ss) and German learners of French (6 Ss) were asked to retell in French the French version of a North American folk tale which, in Bartlett's experiments (1932 : 64-94), was entitled "The War of the Ghosts" (for a more detailed description of our experiment cf. Geib, 1978). This story is characterized by a specific textual structure (cf. Mandler and Johnson, 1977 : 136-137) that causes some comprehension difficulty for subjects unfamiliar with the structure of American Indian tales. These difficulties, incidentally, were partly confirmed by our own experiment, as well by the L1 as by the L2 speakers; however, our main concern here will be those difficulties and resulting strategies that may reasonably be claimed to be typical of the German learners' planning processes.

We would like to postulate that there are qualitative differences between native speakers and L2 learners in the planning, execution, and correction of their speech. As a first illustration we take passages which engage the problem of indirect discourse. It is of minor psycholinguistic significance and certainly not surprising to find that native speakers show a greater variety in the use of reporting verbs (*dire, répondre, demander, raconter, prétexter, proposer, avertir*, etc.) than L2 learners, who often resorted to monotonous sequences in the use of the verb *dire*. But of greater interest is the observation that the native speakers of French most commonly made indirect discourse depend on a single verb even when the quotation consisted of a lengthy utterance. The learners of French, however, with great regularity used a verb for every single statement. This result may indicate that the scope of planning and monitoring in the second language was limited compared with that of L1 (Geib, 1978 : 109). More generally speaking, passages with a high processing load — in this case complex constructions containing several dependent clauses — led more easily to planning difficulties in L2 than in L1 productions. Here is one example taken from a German storyteller (silent pauses are indicated by /):

(1) il racontait par exemple que ces gens-là / qui / euhm que ces gens-là étaient / des fantômes parce qu'il ne pouvait pas c... / euh comprendre euhm (sigh) /// al... alors ce jeune homme ne pouvait pas du tout comprendre que les autres lui ont dit qu'il était blessé ou abattu.

In any case, as was to be expected, the use of indirect discourse caused more trouble for the second language learners than the use of direct discourse. This can be deduced from the significant increase of hesitation phenomena, such as filled pauses, false starts, repeats or corrections, immediately before or at the beginning of the indirect discourse. Occasionally a speaker even changed from indirect discourse to direct:

(2) soudain un de ces guerriers disait // que // il d... il disait regardez les [...] (Geib, 1978 : 108).

This example leads to the general concept of 'avoidance strategy' in second language performance. Avoidance strategy presupposes the anticipation of planning problems in the act of speaking (cf. Dechert, 1979). The following passage with the self-correction of *arrivaient* is an example:

(3) quand les guerriers et l'un de ces jeunes hommes étaient arrivés à la ville de Kalama les gens de cette ville / arrivaient allai... allaient jusqu'à la rive de / de cette rivière et les guerriers / commençaient le combat.

To be sure, avoidance strategy is not restricted to second language performance; there are, however, some particular factors that determine its quality and its effect in L2 performance, such as the second-language-learning methods to which the individual speaker has been exposed and the degree of linguistic competence he has reached in L2.

In spite of such personal variables, there were striking similarities in certain forms of speech behavior throughout the L2 productions in our experiment. Several German story-tellers showed, for example, a tendency to string together words of similar meaning, as if they were not sure which one was appropriate. This seems to be, in cases of uncertainty, a popular strategy with which the learner tries to improve the chances for the listener to understand the intended message properly. Here is one of those examples:

(4) et euh le jeune homme euh raconte son avent... aventure euh / à ses parents à ses proches à ses voisins / .

Together with similar forms of speech behavior (cf. Seliger in this volume) strings of this kind may also supply some information about lexical storage in second language speakers.

In addition to special features occasioned by difficulties in planning on the syntactical and lexical level, we also found evidence in almost all L2 performances of problems that concerned the level of the text: the L2 learners usually had trouble assigning textual coherence to their productions. This deficiency, which manifested itself in the lack of connectives and of certain pronouns, does not seem to be crucially dependent on the specific episodic structure of the story to be retold; the passages in question reveal, for example, that there obviously existed a general uncertainty among the German story-tellers about the 'scope' of pronouns, i.e. the second language learners were not sure when to refer to already mentioned persons or objects in form of pronouns or nouns. Together with the notorious difficulty German learners generally find in the use of French pronouns, this uncertainty led to an extensive use of literal repetitions — obviously another form of avoidance strategy. This is one of the reasons why the L2 productions conveyed the impression of being much more monotonous and redundant than the L1 performances (for the notion of simplification strategies in this connection cf. Corder and Roulet, 1977). The following passage might be instructive:

(5) là il voyaient s'approcher un canoë / et dans ce canoë ils voyaient cinq hommes et quand les cinq hommes dans le canoë étaient arrivés...

There is another genuinely psychological approach to the comparison of speech performance of the type described in this section. As we mentioned above, it is assumed that the structure of the chosen American Indian story is understood only with difficulty by subjects unfamiliar with the special schema developed there. In this connection, Kintsch and van Dijk (1978 : 64) take up the notion of the macro-structure: "the global organization of the semantic structure of a discourse." It organizes "both the production and the comprehension, storage and recall of complex verbal structures such as discourses." Their experiments with native speakers provide evidence for the hypothesis that knowledge of the appropriate narrative schema is a necessary condition for understanding, and hence summarizing, the text. It may be assumed that these findings are relevant for the reproductions of native speakers and of second language learners as well. If the right narrative schema were available, L2 productions would probably be better organized and more 'fluent' than if the organization of the story were obscure and no story grammar were available. The arrangement of our own experiment with its restriction to one story does not allow an evaluation of this hypothesis; but a detailed analysis of the obtained speech performance might provide some material for tentative answers to questions which refer to the cognitive processes involved in comprehension of the text and production of L2 learners. For example, 1. If, in accordance with findings of Kintsch and others (cf. Tulving and Donaldson, 1972), the memory for verbal utterances is predominantly semantic for native speakers, then, is it also semantic to the same extent for L2 learners? or, to put it differently, do second language learners have a stronger tendency to take up expressions and linguistic structures that they remember from the original story? 2. What transformations or substitutions do speakers impose on elements of the story which were hard for them to understand, especially for cultural reasons?

Other elicitation tasks are, of course, conceivable without being limited to storytelling, to provide valuable information about the influence of differences in cognitive style and of cultural differences on speech performance processes. Some of Fathman's comparisons reported in this volume may serve as examples. Another illustration is the interesting experiment made by Haggan (1973), who compared the productions of Arabic speaking learners of English: One group was allowed to practise discussing a topic in their native language, before discussing it in English, the other group was not. Haggan found "an improvement in output in terms of quality of ideas and syntactic accuracy, as compared with non-practised target language speech."

To conclude this section, we believe that differences between the mental processes of people speaking their native language and groups of learners of that language constitute an attractive domain of research for what we have named contrastive psycholinguistics. Cross-linguistic studies of the type described in this section may be regarded as a promising approach for the discovery of characteristic differences in planning processes and verbal strategies.

3. *Characteristics of Individual Second Language Learners*

The number and distribution of certain forms of speech behavior may vary considerably from one second language learner to another, even for the same given task. To integrate such idiosyncrasies into a theory of second language speech performance, cross-linguistic comparisons of an individual's performance in his native language with his production in the target language turn out to be very useful.

As to the frequency and distribution of some temporal variables we can refer to results of our own comparisons of L1 and L2 productions of individual speakers (Raupach, forthcoming). In their L1 descriptions of a cartoon, some of the German and French students differed markedly from their fellow speakers in the two respective groups, not only in their pausal profile, including variables such as speaking and articulation rate, ratio of pause-time, length of runs, etc. (cf. above Table 2), but also in the use of 'parenthetical remarks'. Curiously enough, the L2 descriptions that the same speaker gave of the same cartoon were characterized, to a large extent, by exactly the same tendencies in temporal organization that was revealed in their respective native language performances: learners who delivered the most fluent L1 descriptions belonged, in fact, to the group of relatively fluent L2 speakers; similarly, the less fluent L1 speakers showed signs of hesitancy and speech disfluencies in their L2 descriptions comparable to their first language performance. This corresponding verbal behavior within the framework of temporal variables was, in nearly all cases, remarkably consistent and was not limited to the temporal patterning in a restricted sense, but affected as well the use of certain 'fillers' or 'parenthetical remarks' in both languages.

The fact that the over-all structures of the individuals' L1 and L2 descriptions generally resembled each other, is not too surprising in view of the specific task (the L2 version had to be given immediately after the L1 description), although there were some interesting discrepancies, obviously due to lexical problems. But this resemblance may perhaps also be taken as supportive of the assumption that the individual's general 'schema' of cartoon descriptions is valid in his first language as well as in his second language. All — and only — those speakers, for example, who had assigned to their L1 descriptions a structure based upon spatial organization (divided into foreground, background, etc.) used the same categories in their L2 performance. We should mention in passing that only French students chose this special form of structuring their productions, which is probably a consequence of their great familiarity with the task of describing pictures.

However, not only are intellectual factors responsible for characteristic forms of a learner's speech behavior; other parameters of L2 learning behavior may, for example, lead to Seliger's distinction (in this volume) between *High Input Generators* (HIG) and *Low Input Generators* (LIG). Here we wish to turn to idiosyncrasies not easily inferred from the speaker's speech behavior in his native language. We can take as another example various types of learners. Seliger (in this volume) contends that learners are either 'primarily planners' or 'correctors'. The justification of this distinction was confirmed in one of our own experiments with German adult learners of French who had to retell a French short story. But even for those speakers who are most clearly representative of these two types of L2 learning, there was, as far as we could see, no clear evidence for an interdependence between their L2 strategies and their native language speech behavior. One illuminating case study revealed, for example, that the learner's L2 production was marked by an excessive use of hesitation phenomena, such as pauses and self-corrections, whereas her L1 performance showed no signs of such an undue use of comparable behaviors. The hesitancies in the L2 production made possible a high degree of idiomatic, organized second language speech; according to her own explanation, the learner was not so much preoccupied with the problem of making herself understood, but rather found great pleasure in rephrasing parts of her production and in looking for better and more idiomatic expressions for use in her speech. We were able to confirm her explanation by a detailed analysis of her performance. Hence, some verbal strategies, largely independent of L1 speech habits, may apparently result from the individual's attitude towards the foreign language and may ultimately be found to be indicators of one's linguistic competence in certain domains of the second language.

It is our hope that this section has already made clear that the proposed cross-linguistic studies of L1 and L2 performance of individual speakers do not aim primarily at an inventory of interferences derived from grammatical and lexical differences between the two languages involved. It cannot be denied, of course, that differences, as well as similarities, exert a strong influence on the learner's

L2 performance; but for contrastive psycholinguistics the proposed type of cross-linguistic comparison is useful, in the first place, to analyze the individual's L2 planning processes and strategies in light of his L1 speech behavior and of other personal factors.

Conclusions

It goes without saying that production processes are closely related to mechanisms relevant to the perception of language. For this reason, we consider the analysis of speech performance a promising method of discovering mental processes that are generally involved in human ability to use language. In addition, the psycholinguistic study of L1 and L2 performance — to concentrate on our main objective — allows the formulation and evaluation of interesting hypotheses for a theory of second language learning.

In our opinion, the most stimulating proposals that can be derived from L1 and L2 speech comparison refer to the differentiation of native speaker's and second language learner's planning and production behavior. Much investigation is still needed to account for the striking similarities that exist between particular forms of speech behavior typical of L2 learners and certain forms of simplification that can be found in productions of native speakers who use non-standard variations. These parallels deserve detailed description and explanation. There remains, nonetheless, strong evidence for the existence of particularities which are reserved for L2 performance only. We assume that learners who share the same native language and cultural background show similar forms of strategies in overcoming difficulties in the comprehension and production of a second language. Apart from this, a person's verbal behavior in L2 is, of course, influenced by a set of individual factors likewise responsible for his personal profile in L1 behavior; other individual factors lead to special strategies that allow a categorization into different types of 'planners' in second language behavior.

There are some demands to be made if one expects cross-linguistic descriptions to contribute to an evaluation of hypotheses regarding the nature of processes underlying speech production of second language learners. As we have stated above, the categories of description should not be temporal variables and hesitation phenomena alone: all possible indicators of planning processes, such as self-corrections or speech errors, should be accounted for. These 'anomalies' must not be analyzed primarily as statistical measures, but rather their occurrence and distribution should lead to plausible interpretations in light of preformulated hypotheses. Such an evaluation procedure cannot be based on narrowly defined linguistic structures like the sentence; there are more relevant levels of description to be taken into consideration, such as the organization of the grammatical and semantic structure of the produced text, which partly reflects the speaker's command of adequate verbal strategies and the availability of an appropriate schema necessary for the accomplishment of a given task.

Further studies of the type described in this article obviously demand the collection of data that allow differentiation among text genre, situations, etc. as well as among individual variables of a speaker. To meet these demands, more case studies are needed; they may provide, in addition, useful material for the description of various stages in the development of an individual's speech behavior.

In our view, a theory of second language learning that ignores the results of speech comparisons in the framework of contrastive psycholinguistics disregards a valuable source of information.

REFERENCES

APPEL, G., H.W. Dechert, and M. Raupach. 1980. *A Selected Bibliography of Temporal Variables in Speech.* Tübingen: Narr.

BARTLETT, F.C. 1932. *Remembering. A Study in Experimental and Social Psychology.* Cambridge: Cambridge University Press.

CAIRNS, H.S. and Ch. E. Cairns. 1976. *Psycholinguistics. A Cognitive View of Language.* New York: Holt, Rinehart and Winston.

CLARK, H.H. 1971. The Importance of Linguistics for the Study of Speech Hesitations. In: D.L. Horton and J.J. Jenkins (eds.). *The Perception of Language.* Columbus, Ohio: Charles E. Merrill, 69-78.

CLARK, H.H. and E.V. Clark. 1977. *Psychology and Language: An Introduction to Psycholinguistics.* New York: Harcourt, Brace, and Jovanovich.

CORDER, S.P. and E. Roulet (eds.). 1977. The Notions of Simplifications, Interlanguages and Pidgins and their Relation to Second Language Pedagogy. *Actes du 5ème colloque de linguistique appliquée de Neuchâtel*, 20-22 mai 1976. Neuchâtel, Genève: Droz.

DECHERT, H.W. 1979. On the Evaluation of 'Avoidance Strategies' in Second-Language Speech Productions. Paper presented at the TESOL Summer Meeting 1979. Los Angeles.

DECHERT, H.W. and M. Raupach (eds.). forthcoming. *Temporal Variables in Speech.* The Hague: Mouton.

FROMKIN, V.A. 1971. The Non-Anomalous Nature of Anomalous Utterances. *Language.* 47, 27-52.

FROMKIN, V.A. (ed.) 1973. *Speech Errors as Linguistic Evidence.* The Hague: Mouton.

GARRETT, M.F. 1975. The Analysis of Sentence Production. In: G.H. Bower (ed.). *The Psychology of Learning and Motivation.* Vol. 9. New York: Academic Press, 133-177.

GEIB, G. 1978 (unpublished). *Probleme der Sprachplanung in Französisch als L2 im Kontext einer Nacherzählung.* Kassel.

GROSJEAN, F. forthcoming. Comparative Studies of Temporal Variables in Spoken and Sign Languages: A Short Review. In: H.W. Dechert and M. Raupach (eds.). *Temporal Variables in Speech.* The Hague: Mouton.

GROSJEAN, F. and A. Deschamps. 1975. Analyse contrastive des variables temporelles de l'anglais et du français: vitesse de parole et variables composantes, phénomènes d'hésitation. *Phonetica*. 31, 144-184.

HAGGAN, M. 1973. *Cross Linguistic Aspects of Pausing*. Ph.D. Thesis. University College London.

KINTSCH, W. and T.A. van Dijk. 1978. Cognitive Psychology and Discourse: Recalling and Summarizing Stories. In: W.U. Dressler (ed.). *Current Trends in Text Linguistics*. Berlin: de Gruyter, 61-80.

KOLERS, P.A. 1963. Interlingual Word Associations. *Journal of Verbal Learning and Verbal Behavior*. 2, 291-300.

MANDLER, J.M. and N.S. Johnson. 1977. Remembrance of Things Parsed: Story Structure and Recall. *Cognitive Psychology*. 9, 111-151.

MARTIN, J.G. 1971. Some Acoustic and Grammatical Features of Spontaneous Speech. In: D.L. Horton and J.J. Jenkins (eds.). *The Perception of Language*. Columbus, Ohio: Charles E. Merrill, 47-68.

MIRON, M.S. and S. Wolfe. 1964. A Cross-Linguistic Analysis of the Response Distributions of Restricted Word Associations. *Journal of Verbal Learning and Verbal Behavior*. 3, 376-384.

PÜRSCHEL, H. 1975. *Pause und Kadenz*. Interferenzerscheinungen bei der englischen Intonation deutscher Sprecher. Tübingen: Niemeyer.

RAUPACH, M. forthcoming. Temporal Variables in First and Second Language Speech Production. In: H.W. Dechert and M. Raupach (eds.). *Temporal Variables in Speech*. The Hague: Mouton.

ROSENZWEIG, M.R. 1961. Comparisons Among Word-Association Responses in English, French, German, and Italian. *American Journal of Psychology*. 74, 347-360.

RUSSELL, W.A. and O.R. Meseck. 1959. Der Einfluß der Assoziation auf das Erinnern von Worten in der deutschen, französischen und englischen Sprache. *Zeitschrift für experimentelle und angewandte Psychologie*. 6, 191-211.

TULVING, E. and W. Donaldson (eds.). 1972. *Organization of Memory*. New York: Academic Press.

CROSS-LINGUISTIC INVESTIGATION OF SOME TEMPORAL DIMENSIONS OF SPEECH

Daniel C. O'Connell
University of Kansas

The following essay can hardly lay claim to engaging the scientific investigation of all temporal factors in speech. The domain it does engage is that of pause and hesitation phenomena. The concern is not with analyses at the level of acoustic phonetics, but rather with analyses at the level of discourse. Typically, the temporal phenomena included in such considerations are silent or unfilled pauses (UPs), filled pauses, repeats, false starts, parenthetical remarks, and drawls or syllabic prolongations. An operational description of all but the last of these measures is given by Kowal, O'Connell, and Sabin (1975 : 198):

> The minimum length of UPs was 270 msec. They were defined by length alone and therefore included also whatever juncture pauses exceeded 270 msec. Filled pauses (FPs) were defined as *uh, ah*, and *hm*. Repeats (Rs) were defined as in Maclay and Osgood (1959). Because of the danger of arbitrary designation, false starts (FSs) were defined according to these conventions: (1) correction of a noun phrase (e.g., *then the dog then the girl)*; (2) correction of a word (e.g., *Now he's let leavin' home)*; and (3) incomplete utterances (e.g., *Snoopy uh has a is about to leave*). Parenthetical remarks (PRs) were defined as in Levin and Silverman (1965). They included words which were considered to function as verbal fillers rather than to convey information (e.g., *well, you know,* and *sort of*).

In actual practice, a vast array of methodologies and instrumentations are used by various investigators to study these phenomena. Other measures are frequently derived from these as well: percentages, ratios, and the like. By all these means it is hoped that the acceleration and retardation of spoken discourse and its detailed pattern and structure can be illuminated.

More specifically, the cross-linguistic study of these temporal phenomena, i.e., their investigation across a variety of natural languages, indulges the general hypothesis that there must be both commonalities and differences in these regards among the languages.

The most basic rationale for the hypothesis of commonalities across languages is to be found in the human vocal instrumentation of speech. The same neurophysiological lawfulness governs not only breathing and articulation, but even thinking and conceptualization across all languages. But there is more. We all dwell within the same spatiotemporal continuum. And despite the theorizing of both absolute and relative Whorfians, the conceptual and affective contents of human communication are sharable and shared across languages.

Nonetheless, some differences can be hypothesized with no less compelling argumentation. The various language communities are distinguishable one from another at many levels. From language to language, cultural traditions and current experiences vary. Factors as varied as gene pool, climate, diet, and occupation characterize language communities, and they are separated by syllabic, syntactic, lexical, phonetic, and other differences as well.

We are left, therefore, with a very complex set of reasons for sameness and difference among languages in their temporal dimensions. Hence there arises, antecedent to all considerations of specific hypotheses or experimental designs, the necessity for a concept of multidetermination. Any functional system as complex as human communication must be expected to manifest some mandatory and some optimal functional tactics.

Some Methodological Comments

Let me exemplify this need for a concept of multidetermination by citing a methodological error made by Hänni (1974). He argues that, if extraneous auditory input during silent pauses fails to disrupt ongoing speech, these same silent pauses cannot be serving the function of planning periods for the speech to follow immediately thereafter. The hypothesis has merit and should not be dismissed lightly; but it is poorly formulated and poorly tested in the research in question. First of all, the silent pauses could well serve the planning function in an optional fashion; but this function could well be shifted to speech time, except under conditions of severe urgency or time limitation. Suffice it to say that such conditions were neither considered relevant nor tested in the Hänni research.

But there is an even more serious flaw in the methodology. Hänni studied only one dimension of silent pauses: their mean length. He did not consider at all their frequency or their positioning or patterning in the discourse. The argument is somewhat like that of a youngster who squeezes one end of a balloon and exclaims: "Look! I made it smaller." Obviously, the balloon has simply betaken itself elsewhere. Similarly, tremendous variation is possible within the silent-pause system of a given corpus of speech, without the slightest change in the mean length of silent pauses. Two pauses of 800 msec in length, for example, are certainly not functionally equivalent to one pause of 300 msec and another of 1300 msec; similarly, a pause between a noun and its adjectival modifier is not functionally equivalent to a pause between sentences. It is hardly warranted, therefore, on the basis of the evidence to say that Hänni "showed that the experimental disruption of pauses does not impede the planning activities supposedly going on during these intervals" (Hörmann, 1978 : 143). It is quite possible in this instance that the planning process underwent a considerable disruptive shift — just like the balloon. But Hänni had no way of knowing whether or not such was the case without looking at the other end of the balloon, the other dimensions of pauses.

Any valid comparison across natural language systems must have as an absolute minimum a comparable data base in each of the languages to be compared. This requirement sounds so basic as to be trivial as well as easily satisfied. But it is neither. The data base must be adequate to be representative of the language in question in such a way that its characteristics cannot be attributable to speech genre, individual differences in speakers, random variation, experimental instructions, or any other identifiable confounding variable. It is a question of careful experimental control and design or, in the case of naturalistic observation, of alertness to the possible operation of such factors.

In order to exemplify problems arising from the data base, I wish to give an extended case history. It makes use of a set of data from Barik (1973; 1975; 1977) which have been subjected to an extraordinary amount of analysis and have been presented in many forms. It is quite true that Barik was preoccupied with questions regarding the characteristics of both simultaneous translation and various speech genre; but at the same time, he does conclude at the very end of his long series of publications that the data "point to a consistency in the temporal characteristics of speech across languages, and provide a basis for further research" (1977 : 126).

In Table 1, one set of response measures derived from Barik's (1977 : 120) data base are summarized. They are not intended to adequately reflect the vast array of analyses presented by the author, but only to provide for the reader a simple framework from which we can begin our discussion of the data base itself.

Table 1

Speech Duration (Percentage Exclusive of Pause Duration)
for English and French Texts
(from Barik, 1977 : 120)

Speech Type	English	French
TAT story	51.2	43.5
Film story	71.1	56.9
Lecture	75.1	81.6
Speech	55.5	67.4
Reading	70.2	71.6

The most important thing to be noted in Table 1 is that each of these percentages is a classical case of $N = 1$. Each entry represents the idiosyncratic performance of one subject. Some subjects are indeed represented in Table 1 by multiple entries, but not in a systematic way within and across languages:

> All recordings were made by adult male native speakers of the language in question. For the English texts, the same speaker recorded the story and the written text, while the other texts were each rendered by a different speaker; for the French passage, all texts except the lecture were rendered by the same speaker (p. 117).

The question that now arises is whether there is any way of isolating the contribution of English and French, respectively, to these percentages. One could, of course, average each column in Table 1 and find that the English and French means differ by only 0.4 % (64.6 and 64.2), but we should not do so before looking at the individual pairs of entries, unless we wish to indulge in numerology.

The English and French TAT stories were based on the same picture and present no additional problems. In the film stories, however, "the speaker was asked to discuss a film that he had recently seen" (Barik, 1977 : 117). No provision was made for possible recency effects or effects due to the nature of the stimulus material constituted by the specific film seen by the respective speakers; "but the two film discussions differed considerably, the English text being 'rougher' than the French text and being characterized by retraces, repetitions, and hesitations on the part of the speaker" (p. 117). The English and French lectures are also problematic: "They did however differ in mode of delivery, the delivery of the French speaker being faster and possibly more difficult to follow" (1973 : 241). (In passing, one might imagine that these differences surely rendered the two lectures poorly controlled materials for purposes of comparison of simultaneous translations). A much more serious problem arises regarding the English and French versions of the speech: "This material consisted of a live recording of a formal non-technical speech in English, for which a formal translation was available in French" (1977 : 117). So far, so good; but "this translation was recorded by a French speaker, who was asked to render it in the same tone and manner as the original" (p. 117). Now imitation of the "manner" of the original could quite reasonably have been construed by the French speaker to include the temporal dimensions of the English speech. Under this supposition, the imitation by the French speaker could well have produced the 67.4 % speech duration for French speech, not as a function of the characteristics of French language speakers as such, but simply as a function of the requested mimesis. In other words, the experimenter came very close to requesting the subject to give him the experimental effect he wished to obtain. Finally, for the readings, the instructions were "to deliver the text in a communicative fashion, with appropriate halts in their delivery, rather than a straight uninterrupted reading" (p. 117). Once again, an instructional set ("appropriate halts" and not "straight uninterrupted reading") rather than simply the characteristics of the respective languages must be suspected of influencing the speech duration percentages for readings in both French and English in Table 1.

If one now returns to Table 1, it should be clear that most of the entries cannot legitimately be considered to represent performance characteristics of the language in which the speaking was done. In fact, only the TAT stories remain above suspicion.

In addition to a valid data base, it is also necessary to have a common methodology and consistent instrumentation across languages for purposes of comparison. The confusion occasioned by failures to adhere to this requirement in pausological studies in general and in cross-linguistic studies in particular has been emphasized in the literature (O'Connell and Kowal; in press; de Johnson, O'Connell and Sabin, 1979). There is, as yet, little comparability on this score from laboratory to laboratory or even from experiment to experiment within the same laboratory.

In order to illustrate these problems more concretely, some data have been selected from studies by Hanley, Snidecor, and Ringel (1966) and Hanley and Snidecor (1967) and are presented in Table 2.

Table 2

Mean Phonation/time Ratios for Males (Hanley, Snidecor and Ringel, 1966 : 101, 103) and Females (Hanley and Snidecor, 1967 : 145)

Task	Sex	Language			
		Tagalog	Spanish	Japanese	American English
Reading	M		.60	.56	.63
	F	.476	.516	.372	.442
Speaking	M		.39	.48	.61

The data for male readers were presented by the authors as nonsignificantly different one from another. The data for male speakers were presented as significantly different at the .01 level but suspect because of heterogeneity of variance, which in turn was hypothesized to be due to some very short (15 sec) samples.

The data for female readers were presented as significantly different at the .01 level one from another. No data were presented on female speakers. The reading material was in each instance the Rainbow Passage (Fairbanks, 1940) translated into the native language of the speaker. The speaking was elicited by a "question designed to elicit spontaneous speech of a like propositional nature" (Hanley et al., 1966 : 98). This "question" is further specified as follows:

> He was further instructed that upon the conclusion of his reading he was to commence speaking spontaneously in his native language about his future career plans, using a "normal conversational manner", for about one minute (pp. 99-100).

Superficially the data of Hanley and his colleagues in Table 2 would appear to be unrelated to the data of Barik in Table 1; nonetheless the logical rationale for the data in both tables is the same. In both, actual speech on-time is expressed as a percentage of the total duration of time from start to finish. The portion of time excluded is the pause time. The fact that the researchers expressed their data as percentages and decimals, in Table 1 and Table 2, respectively, is unimportant.

But, although the data are conceptually the same, the operational procedures from which they were derived were very different. Hanley and his colleagues used no cut-off point at all in measuring pause time. Barik (1973 : 244) used a cut-off point of 610 msec; all pauses of < 610 msec were discounted and thereby automatically included in the speech on-time category. We will come back to the generic question of cut-off points and their methodological importance somewhat later. For the moment, however, the point to be made is a concrete one regarding the research exemplified in Tables 1 and 2. The discrepancy regarding the use of a cut-off point renders the data in the two tables incompatible for purposes of comparison. For example, all of Barik's on-time percentages for reading are higher than all the corresponding entries for reading in Table 2.

But there are other methodological and instrumentation problems that affect the data in Table 2. Hanley and Snidecor (1967) found that a high ambient noise level made it necessary for them to arrive at instrumental measurements of phonation/time ratio for some of the female readers (unidentified as to which language groups they might have belonged to) "individually for each subject" (p. 145). The authors added: "The degree of error introduced by this system cannot be assessed" (p. 145). Perhaps the acknowledged uncertainty about the accuracy of some of the 1967 data accounts for the fact that there are very few comparisons made in the 1967 study with the 1966 research. The remarkable diminution in phonation/time ratios in female readers relative to male readers might suggest that there was indeed an instrumental constant error due to some of the female readers' ratios. Otherwise, significant differences across the languages for the female readers, when no differences at all are in evidence for the male readers, are not understandable or even plausible.

Hanley and Snidecor's (1967) summary comment to the effect that "Tagalog proved to have a relatively high phonation/time ratio, whereas American English and Japanese had low ratios" (p. 147) is positively misleading in light of the data themselves. As may be noted from Table 2, Spanish readers, not Tagalog readers, had the highest mean phonation/time ratio among female subjects (the 1967 data). The numerical value of the Tagalog mean phonation/time ratio (.476) was actually closer to that of the American English female readers (.442) than any other one in the entire table. The authors simply did not summarize their results properly.

In summary, Tables 1 and 2 and the accompanying commentary illustrate the extraordinary caution required in interpreting response measures in cross-linguistic comparisons. The problems associated with small (or short), unreliable samples, methodological conventions, instrumentation, cutt-off points, biased stimulus materials, biased instructions, and other artifactual elements are legion.

An empirical and methodological study of "Artifacts in the registration and interpretation of speech-process variables" by Braehler and Zenz (1975) has done us all a great service in this respect with its frank analysis of artifacts. What Braehler and Zenz refer to as "the uncritical usage of variables as being synonymous with semantic concepts" (p. 167) has indeed led to a great deal of confusion in cross-linguistic as well as other comparisons. We can refer to only a few of their more important conclusions here, while recommending their entire article to researchers who have not as yet noted it. From their observations they conclude:

> owing to intrinsic limitations in the use of technical equipment, the selection of a minimum time-unit in pause-analysis is unavoidable; at the same time, however, we must point out that interpretative implications, such as "hesitation pauses" or "articulatory pauses" should be carefully guarded against, as this reduces the field of association and narrows the range of vision for subsequent research-work (p. 170).

More specifically with regard to a cut-off point for pauses, they add succinctly "the selection of a cut-off point for pauses directly determines one's conclusions as to the length of pauses or number of words per chunk" (p. 171).

Levels of Proficiency

Ironically enough, one of the earliest cross-linguistic studies is exemplary both in its methodology and in its data base across six languages: English, French, German, Italian, Latin, and Greek. Cattell's (1885, 1886) research should not be dismissed simply as historically quaint or as procedurally clever. Using a simple stopwatch to time subjects who were asked to read as fast as possible, he concluded:

> The rate at which a person reads a foreign language is proportional to his familiarity with the language. For example, when reading as fast as possible the writer's rate was, English 138, French 167, German 250, Italian 327, Latin 434 and Greek 484; the figures giving the thousandths of a second taken to read each word. Experiments made on others strikingly confirm these results. The subject does not know that he is reading the foreign language more slowly than his own; this explains why foreigners seem to talk so fast. This simple method of determining a person's familiarity with a language might be used in school-examinations (1886 : 65).

The basic insight that measurable temporal phenomena in human speech reflect level of proficiency in one's native language as well as in foreign languages has far-reaching implications that have been largely neglected in the intervening century of research. Cattell found only negligible differences in rate between native speakers of English and German as such (1885 : 648-649).

It is not the case, of course, that "foreigners seem to talk so fast" simply because we are not able to speak a foreign language in question quite as fast as they. Cattell's logic is a bit elliptical at this point. There is obviously a perceptual component in our unfamiliarity with a foreign language. We are unable to perceive the speech sounds of a language less familiar than our native language as quickly as we are able to perceive the speech sounds of the native language itself.

Another way of making use of proficiency level to provide cross-language comparisons is exemplified in research by O'Connell (1969). The first part of the study was a replication with native speakers of German (all of whom knew English) of research by O'Connell, Turner and Onuska (1968, Experiment I) originally carried out with native speakers of American English. The design involved immediate recall of strings of 15 nonsense syllables of English speech sounds. The strings also simulated English morphological and syntactic structure at three levels: no structure, low structure (morphology alone), and high structure (morphology and syntax). They were presented orally, either monotonously or with intonation.

Table 3 presents the mean length of oral recall time (in sec) on the last five trials in both experiments;

Table 3

Mean Recall Time (Averaged in Sec per Subject Over Trials 21-25) for Immediate Recall of 15 Nonsense Syllables by Native Speakers of English (O'Connell, Turner and Onuska, 1968 : 113) and German (O'Connell, 1969 : 42), Respectively

Condition	English	German
Monotone, no structure	14.5	16.6
Monotone, low structure	13.8	16.4
Monotone, high structure	11.6	12.1
Intonated, no structure	9.5	7.8
Intonated, low structure	8.4	10.3
Intonated, high structure	6.1	6.0

earlier trials were omitted because the recall did not in every instance include 15 syllables. In both English and German subjects, intonation and structure produced significant decreases in recall time. The reader will note, however, in Table 3 that low structure was not facilitative for the native speakers of German.

O'Connell's (1969) comment was as follows:

> The difficulty of the low structure condition for non-native speakers of English seems to parallel the difficulty experienced by native speakers of English with the same condition in the Bryk (1968) research. In his research, the difficulty was ascribed to the negative transfer due to unsyntactic order. This negative influence was manifest only when the nonsense-stems were of low meaningfulness (unwordlike). It would appear plausible to suggest that the low structure condition occurs precisely because his relative lack of familiarity with English renders nonsense-stems less wordlike or meaningful for him than for a native speaker. This difficulty would, of course, be contributed to by his tendency (because of his native language habits) to construe the stems as German (p. 46).

Differences in temporal dimensions due to levels of proficiency *across* languages lead fairly straightforwardly to the hypothesis of analogous differences *within* a given language; specifically, it is plausible that age-related changes in language skills produce changes in temporal dimensions of speech within a language. Some recent research has actually proceeded instead from such within-language hypotheses in age-related research back to hypotheses regarding level of proficiency across languages. O'Connell and Kowal (1972) found that amount and patterning of silent pause time varied dramatically across age from adolescence to adulthood in native speakers of both English and German. Mean number of silent pauses was significantly greater in readings by adolescents than in those by adults; a similar comparison between German and English readers showed no significant differences. Kowal, O'Connell, O'Brien and Bryant (1975) then hypothesized that temporal measures would be sensitive enough to detect differences even within an age range as small as two years, second and fourth grades, in the American elementary school system. The results were encouraging:

> The main effect of age in both reading and storytelling reflected a difference of only two years. Second graders read more slowly than fourth-graders ... the present experiment emphasized efficient use of syntactic units. The increase in reading rate in older subjects was not due to shorter unfilled pauses but only to a smaller number of them ...

> The speech rate in the storytellings was slower for the younger subjects. In contrast to the results found for the readings, the decrease in rate was due to an increase in length but not number of unfilled pauses (pp. 557-558).

It was only at this point that Kowal, O'Connell, O'Brien and Bryant (1975) invoked an analogy of levels of proficiency across languages to age-related differences. Four different levels of proficiency in the use of the German language were sampled: Subjects at the first level had no academic or familial training in German; those at the second level had four to six semesters of college German or the equivalent: those at the third level were graduate students in German language studies; and those at the fourth level were native speakers of German who had lived in an English-speaking country for five years or less. The hypotheses were resoundingly confirmed:

> In the readings, not only did the number of unfilled pauses within major syntactic units or words decrease over increasing levels of proficiency, but the number of unfilled pauses between units decreased too, though not as dramatically. The mean length of these unfilled pauses decreased correspondingly (nonsignificantly for those between units). Consequently, speech rate and phrase length increased with proficiency (p. 552).

It should be noted that the major syntactic units become an important analytic component in the age-related and cross-language experiments. The ability of the subject to unitize and segregate syntactically in performance becomes a crucial test of level of proficiency in the language and is important for the speaker and hearer, respectively, in terms of encoding and decoding a coherent message.

Performance Characteristics of Languages

Quite a different research strategy from the levels of proficiency approach requires comparable levels of proficiency across subjects in order to uncover performance characteristics ascribable to the various language systems themselves. Much of the research of Grosjean and his colleagues, some of which is presented in detail in his chapter in this volume, has pursued this logic.

In comparing French and English, Grosjean and Deschamps (1972; 1973; 1975) found the amount of silent pause time to be generally similar across the two languages, though with different patterning. Dramatic differences occurred, however, in vocal hesitations. The French speakers used many drawls (syllabic prolongations), whereas the English speakers used many filled pauses. de Johnson, O'Connell and Sabin's (1979) results with Spanish and English speakers remarkably parallel these findings: a relative similarity of silent pause rate across the two languages, but differences in vocal hesitations. In the present instance, however, there was a functional equivalence between filled pauses in English and parenthetical remarks in Spanish.

Other reseachers have also found similarities across languages, for the most part in speech rate and in the use of silent pauses. Osser and Peng (1964) found the speech rates of Japanese and American speakers to be quite similar. Black, Tosi, Singh, and Takefuta (1966) found no significant differences in silent pauses used by Hindi, Spanish, and Japanese speakers either in their native tongues or in their English reading.

The most comprehensive sampling to date known to this author has been collected by Glukhov (1975). A total of 35 hours and 50 minutes comprised the sample of Spanish, Portuguese, French, Italian, English, and German, all recorded from live radio broadcasts. The samples for each language, respectively, in hours and minutes were: 8.00, 3.50, 4.00, 5.40, 6.30, and 7.50. His data are shown in Figure 1.

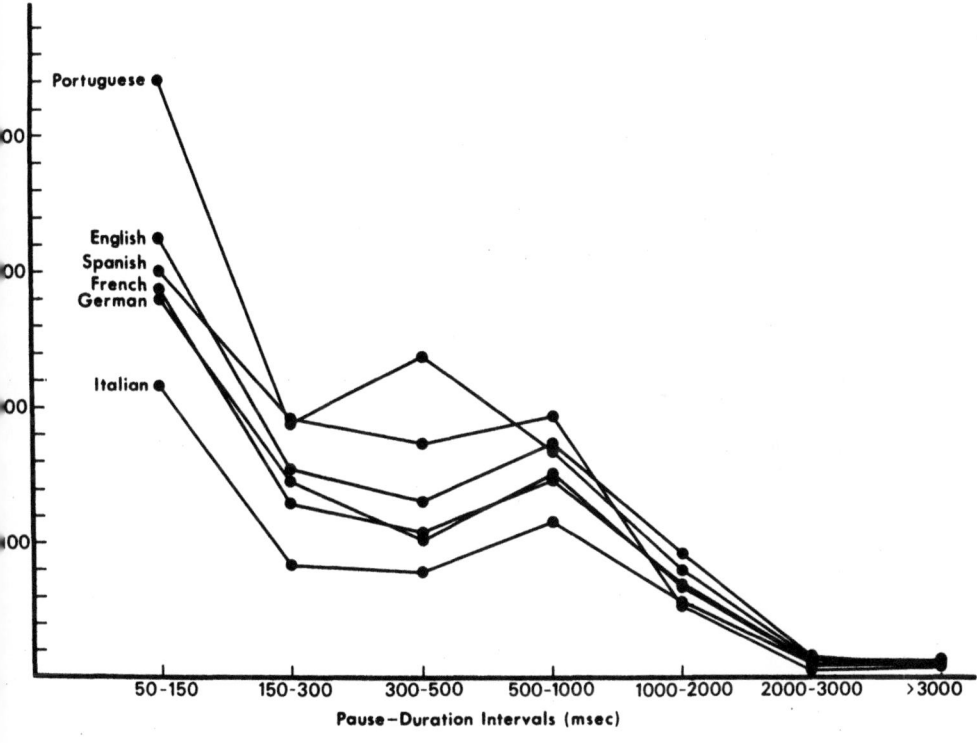

FIGURE 1

Average number of silent pauses per hour over pause-duration intervals for six languages (Glukhov, 1975 : 71)

All pauses < 50 msec in length were disregarded. The following generalizations emerged:

> An analysis of the experimental data implies the existence of a common distribution function governing the off-duty factor of the speech pattern of a talker for the majority of the languages investigated ... the specifics of the different languages have only a relatively slight influence on the univariate pause distribution function (p. 72).

But some differences also emerged: Pause rates for Portuguese, English, Spanish, German, French, and Italian speakers were 3, 4, 4, 5, 5, and 6 per sec, respectively; and the average percentages of pause time over the period of time sampled ranged correspondingly in order of magnitude: 4.2, 4.0, 3.6, 3.4, 3.4, and 2.6, respectively.

These percentages are extraordinarily small in comparison with other samples. Tables 1 and 2 in this chapter, for example, give a vastly different picture of what Glukhov refers to as the off-duty factor (i.e., pause time) of the speech pattern of a talker. One might generalize that the percentage of off-duty time to be expected would be of two digit magnitude. What appears even more anomalous is that most of the studies which yield higher percentages than Glukhov's also use a higher cut-off point for minimum length of silent pauses. Such a higher cut-off point should be expected to yield a shift in the opposite direction, i.e., toward a relatively smaller, not a larger percentage of off-duty time. The argument could be made that Glukhov, unlike nearly all the other researchers, was dealing with broadcast speech. But Szawara and O'Connell (1977), using a relatively conservative cut-off point of 270 msec with broadcast speech, found off-duty time to be 29.4 % (Table 1, p. 361). The discrepancy remains unsolved for this author.

Even though no two of Glukhov's pause-duration intervals are equal, his distributions are of considerable interest. It would appear from Figure 1 that the Portuguese and Italian speakers are the ones who are "singing out of chorus," both with respect to number of silent pauses per hour and patterning across pause-duration intervals. The Portuguese speakers use 225 more and the Italians 188 fewer pauses per hour than any other group; across all four of the other groups the range is only 140. Glukhov himself provided no inferential statistics.

The dominance of shorter pauses in all the languages sampled is not surprising; they presumably comprise mostly between-word pauses (along with even some within-word pauses) which probably "reflect only necessary phonational discontinuities" (O'Connell, Kowal and Hörmann, 1969 : 52). On this score, Glukhov's use of the term "semantic pause" (p. 72) to include even the 50 - 150 msec interval is not felicitous. It is quite likely that their function is largely articulation (Goldman-Eisler, 1968 : 12).

Glukhov's distributions also throw light on the use of longer cut-off points. It is clear, for example, that the use of cut-off points of > 500 msec excludes an appreciable number of silent pauses from the data base — in fact > 70 % of the pauses observed by Glukhov's methods.

A final look at Figure 1 may help us to extrapolate from Glukhov's data a plausible but tentative picture of some pause-duration universals across languages. The greatest differences in frequency of occurrence are to be expected in the shortest interval (50-150 msec) recorded by Glukhov. The average number of silent pauses per hour in Portuguese speakers was almost twice as great (430 > 217) as in Italian speakers; even in this interval, however, the data for the remaining four languages were all within a range of 42. In all the languages studied, the shortest interval contained more silent pauses than any other interval. It is, of course, physically possible for a greater number of shorter pauses than longer pauses to occur within a given period of time, but actual occurrence of silent pauses of < 150 msec in length is most likely due to necessary shifts in articulation of vowels and consonants peculiar to the sound systems of the respective languages. Hence some variation in the frequency of these pauses is to be expected across languages as a function of the sound system peculiar to a given language. The vast majority of the remaining silent pauses in all the languages studied by Glukhov occurred in the 150-2000 msec pause-duration intervals, and therein is the focus of almost all current pausological research. The frequency of occurrence of silent pauses in these intervals can evidently be expected to be similar across languages, and these pauses can most appropriately be designated by Glukhov's term "semantic" pauses. Silent pauses of > 2000 msec are less common but functionally important. They are well suited for expressive, dramatic impact in speech precisely because they last longer and occur less frequently.

Conclusion

Systematic cross-linguistic investigation of temporal dimensions of speech has not enjoyed an auspicious first century. Now that some of the methodological flaws can be put behind us, the time should be ripe for renewed efforts toward a better understanding of the commonalities and differences among languages along temporal dimensions.

Some readers may indeed have found the foregoing chapter inordinately critical of much of the extant cross-linguistic research on temporal dimensions of speech. It is this author's conviction, however, that just the opposite is all too often the case in modern psycholinguistics (and perhaps generally in psychology). It is unfortunate that conclusions presented in respectable journals by respectable scholars are in turn endowed with something very much like middle-class social respectability. Such conclusions need to be questioned again and again instead of being immediately and definitively archivized in introductory textbooks. The research criticized in these pages has not been notably more deficient than research in other content areas within psycholinguistics; it has simply been subjected to more rigorous critique. If the only function the chapter serves is to warn against uncritical acceptance of research findings, it will have served its purpose well.

REFERENCES

BARIK, H.C. 1973. Simultaneous Interpretation: Temporal and Quantitative Data. *Language and Speech.* 16, 237-270.

BARIK, H.C. 1975. Simultaneous Interpretation: Qualitative and Linguistic Data. *Language and Speech.* 18, 272-297.

BARIK, H.C. 1977. Cross-Linguistic Study of Temporal Characteristics of Different Types of Speech Materials. *Language and Speech.* 20, 116-126.

BLACK, J.W., O. Tosi, S. Singh and Y. Takefuta. 1966. A Study of Pauses in Oral Reading of One's Native Language and English. *Language and Speech.* 9, 237-241.

BRAEHLER, E. and H. Zenz. 1975. Artifacts in the Registration and Interpretation of Speech-Process Variables. *Language and Speech.* 18, 166-179.

BRYK, J.A. 1968. *The Influence of Syntax in Rote Verbal Learning.* Paper presented at the meetings of the Psychonomic Society. St. Louis, Missouri. November 1968.

CATTELL, J. McK. 1885. Ueber die Zeit der Erkennung und Benennung von Schriftzeichen, Bildern und Farben. *Philosophische Studien.* 2, 635-650.

CATTELL, J. McK. 1886. The Time it Takes to See and Name Objects. *Mind.* 11, 63-65.

de JOHNSON, T.H., D. C. O'Connell and E.J. Sabin. 1979. Temporal Analysis of English and Spanish Narratives. *Bulletin of the Psychonomic Society.* 13, 347-350.

FAIRBANKS, G. 1940. *Voice and Articulation Drillbook.* New York: Harper.

GLUKHOV, A. A. 1975. Statistical Analysis of Speech Pauses for Romance and Germanic Languages. *Soviet Physics. Acoustics.* 21, 71-72.

GOLDMAN-EISLER, F. 1968. *Psycholinguistics: Experiments in Spontaneous Speech.* London: Academic Press.

GROSJEAN, F. and A. Deschamps. 1972. Analyse des variables temporelles du français spontané. *Phonetica.* 26, 129-156.

GROSJEAN, F. and A. Deschamps. 1973. Analyse des variables temporelles du français spontané. II. Comparaison du français oral dans la description avec l'anglais (description) et avec le français (interview radiophonique). *Phonetica.* 28, 191-226.

GROSJEAN, F. and A. Deschamps. 1975. Analyse contrastive des variables temporelles de l'anglais et du français: vitesse de parole et variables composantes, phénomènes d'hésitation. *Phonetica*. 31, 144-184.

HANLEY, T.D. and J.C. Snidecor. 1967. Some Acoustic Similarities Among Languages. *Phonetica*. 17, 141-148.

HANLEY, T.D., J.C. Snidecor and R.L. Ringel. 1966. Some Acoustic Differences Among Languages. *Phonetica*. 14, 97-107.

HÄNNI, R. 1974. Auswirkungen der Störungen von Sprechpausen. *Bericht über den 28. Kongreß der Deutschen Gesellschaft für Psychologie*. Göttingen: Hogrefe, 169-177.

HÖRMANN, H. 1978. German Psycholinguistics: 1967-1977. *The German Journal of Psychology*. 2, 136-152.

KOWAL, S., D.C. O'Connell, E.A. O'Brien and E.T. Bryant. 1975. Temporal Aspects of Reading Aloud and Speaking: Three Experiments. *American Journal of Psychology*. 88, 549-569.

KOWAL, S., D.C. O'Connell and E.J. Sabin. 1975. Development of Temporal Patterning and Vocal Hesitation in Spontaneous Narratives. *Journal of Psycholinguistic Research*. 4, 195-207.

LEVIN, H. and I. Silverman. 1965. Hesitation Phenomena in Children's Speech. *Language and Speech*. 8, 67-85.

MACLAY, H. and C.E. Osgood. 1959. Hesitation Phenomena in Spontaneous English Speech. *Word*. 15, 19-44.

O'CONNELL, D.C. 1969. Nonsense Strings, Words, and Sentences: Some Cross-Linguistic Comparisons. *Psychologische Forschung*. 33, 37-49.

O'CONNELL, D.C. and S. Kowal. 1972. Cross-Linguistic Pause and Rate Phenomena in Adults and Adolescents. *Journal of Psycholinguistic Research*. 1, 155-164.

O'CONNELL, D.C. and S. Kowal. in press. Pausology. In: W. and S. Sedelow (eds.). *Computer Uses in the Study of Languages*. Vol. III. *Cognitive Approaches*. The Hague: Mouton.

O'CONNELL, D.C., S. Kowal and H. Hörmann. 1969. Semantic Determinants of Pauses. *Psychologische Forschung*. 33, 50-67.

O'CONNELL, D.C., E.A. Turner and L.A. Onuska. 1968. Intonation, Grammatical Structure, and Contextual Association in Immediate Recall. *Journal of Verbal Learning and Verbal Behavior*. 7, 110-116.

OSSER, H. and F. Peng. 1964. A Cross-Cultural Study of Speech Rate. *Language and Speech*. 7, 120-125.

SZAWARA, J. and D.C. O'Connell. 1977. Temporal Reflections of Spontaneity in Homilies. *Bulletin of the Psychonomic Society*. 9, 360-362.

TEMPORAL VARIABLES WITHIN AND BETWEEN LANGUAGES [1]

François Grosjean
Northeastern University
Boston, Mass.

Researchers have long been interested in the temporal variables of language. Although the term 'temporal variables' refers to those variables that pertain to timing in language (utterance rate and duration, frequency and duration of pauses), it has been extended — rightly or wrongly — to include hesitation phenomena such as filled pauses, repeats, drawls, false starts, etc. After a first generation of studies that examined the temporal variables of individual spoken languages (for example, Goldman-Eisler, 1968; Maclay and Osgood, 1959; Blankenship and Kay, 1964; etc.), a great deal of current research is aimed at comparing these variables across languages (see for example, O'Connell and Kowal, 1972; Barik, 1977). The primary aim of these cross-linguistic studies is to uncover those aspects of temporal variables that are language specific and those that are common to language in general.

Our work over the last eight years follows this latter line of research. In the following chapter we will review a number of studies that compare two oral languages, English and French, and one sign language, American Sign Language. After a short presentation of the temporal variables in question, we will examine these variables in French interviews and descriptions. We will then contrast English and French speakers in an interview situation and attempt to account for the main differences that were found between the two languages. This will lead us to the comparison of temporal variables in two different language modalities: speech (English) and sign (American Sign Language), and we will conclude with a section on future perspectives for this type of cross-linguistic research.

1. *A Description of Temporal Variables*

Grosjean (1972), basing himself on previous work by Goldman-Eisler (1968), Kelly and Steer (1949) and Maclay and Osgood (1959), proposed a working de-

---

[1] The preparation of this chapter was supported in part by grant numbers 768 2530, National Science Foundation, and RR 07143, Department of Health, Education and Welfare.

scription of a number of temporal variables. He separated these into primary and secondary variables and into complex and simple variables and showed how the complex variables can be decomposed into a set of simple variables. As this description has been used quite extensively by a number of researchers (Grosjean and Deschamps, 1972, 1973, 1975; Lucci, 1973, 1974; Saint-Bonné and Boë, 1977; Duez, 1976) we will point out its main aspects below.

I. *Primary Variables.* These variables are always present in language output. They can be separated into two types: complex and simple variables, the latter being components of the former.

    A. *Complex Variables.*

    Speaking Rate. This variable is measured in words or syllables per minute and is obtained by dividing the total number of words (or syllables) in the utterance by the total speaking time and multiplying the product by 60.

    Phonation-Time Ratio (P.T.R.). This ratio (usually expressed as a percentage) indicates the amount of time spent articulating during the utterance. It is obtained by dividing the time spent articulating by the total speech time and multiplying the product by 100.

    B. *Simple Variables.*

    Articulation Rate. This is the actual phonation rate of the speaker. It is usually expressed in syllables/sec and is obtained by dividing the number of syllables in the utterance by the speaker's articulation time (total speaking time minus the pause time).

    Length of Silent Pauses. These pauses, also called unfilled pauses or more simply, pauses, are all the silences $\geq 0,25$ sec as measured on a pen recording. Researchers have long been aware that such silences reflect a number of operations (planning, hesitating, breathing, marking a grammatical boundary, marking emphatic stress, etc.), but attempts to separate out these various activities have always proved to be difficult (see Grosjean and Collins, 1979, for example). This is because silence pauses are often the product of a number of operations; for instance, a speaker will mark a grammatical break by inserting a pause but may also use that silence to breathe, plan and/or hesitate. In the following pages we will make no effort to factor out these various operations.

    Length of Runs. As the number of pauses depends on the length of the speech sample, a more appropriate measure is the length of the runs. A run is defined as the speech that occurs between two pauses. It can reflect a word, a phrase, a sentence or a series of sentences depending on the task and the rate of output. Run length is usually measured in syllables.

Figure 1 presents the breakdown of the complex variables into simple variables. It should be noted that the mean length of runs, the number of runs and the number of pauses all reflect the same variable: the frequency of alternations between pausing and articulating. In the following review we will usually refer to the mean length of runs.

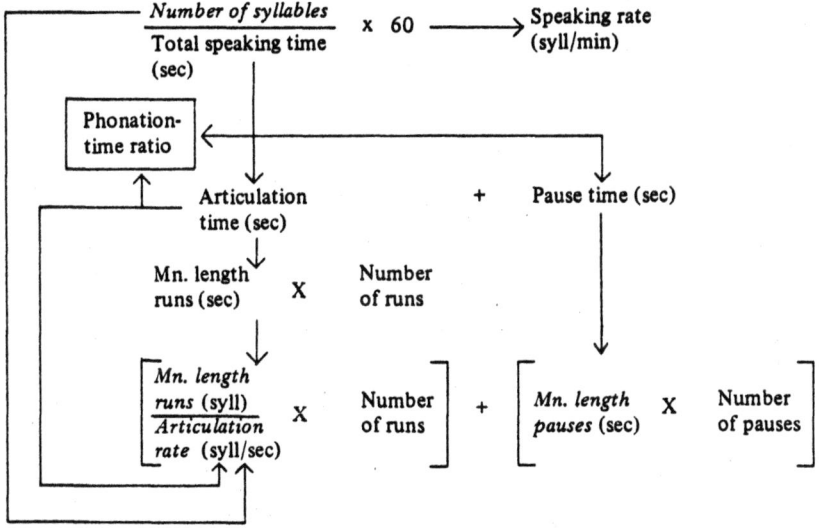

FIGURE 1. The breakdown of complex variables (speaking rate and phonation-time ratio) into simple variables (articulation rate, length of runs and length of pauses). The complex variables are framed and the simple variables italicized.

II. *Secondary Variables*. All these variables belong to the hesitation phenomena category. Unlike the primary variables, their presence is not required in speaking and they rarely occur in oral reading and in very fluent speech. Silent pauses, although classified with the primary variables, may also belong to this second category depending on the type of language uttered; researchers have attempted — unsuccessfully to our mind — to distinguish between fluent and non-fluent silent pauses (the first would belong to the primary variable category and the second to the secondary variables).

Four secondary variables were examined in our studies: filled pauses (such as /ə, ɑ, ɾ, əm /, etc.); drawls (unnatural lengthening of syllables); repeats (any repetition that does not add to the meaning of the utterance) and false starts (any unfinished phrase or sentence).

In our work on American Sign Language the following temporal variables were studied: the signing rate (signs/min), the phonation-time ratio, the articulation rate (signs/sec), the length of pauses (in which the hands are held in the position and configuration of the last sign) and the number of pauses.

2. *Temporal Variables Within a Language: Interviews and Descriptions in French*

Within-language comparisons of temporal variables can be very informative concerning the encoding operations that take place when a speaker is faced with various linguistic tasks: speaking to another person, taking part in a discussion, describing a scene or event, making a speech, etc. The ease with which the speaker can encode his utterances is related (among other things) to the amount of constraint imposed on him by the linguistic task. This in turn is reflected by such variables as speaking rate, number of pauses, amount of hesitation, etc. as Goldman-Eisler (1968) showed when she compared cartoon descriptions and interpretations. Grosjean and Deschamps (1973) were interested in comparing the values of a number of temporal variables across two very different language tasks: taking part in an interview (where the constraint on the speaker is rather light) and describing a series of cartoons (where the constraint is heavier). In addition, they wanted to ascertain the accuracy of the following statement by Goldman-Eisler (1968 : 68), "We take it that descriptions and conversational speech entail, on the average, a similar level of cognitive effort (...) this assumption is supported by the fact that the mean pause time when describing cartoons was not much different from interview pause time, i.e. when no extra intellectual effort is involved."

Twenty students were asked to describe two cartoons; the first contained 8 pictures, the second 3 pictures. Their productions were transcribed and analyzed along the lines spelled out in the previous section. The results were compared to those obtained by Grosjean and Deschamps (1972) who analyzed 30 radio interviews in which speakers were questioned on topics familiar to them.

The results obtained were very different across the two tasks. The speaking rates, for example, were significantly different: 264 syll/min (mean) for the interviews and 153 syll/min for the descriptions. In fact, the two distributions of speaking rates did not overlap: the lowest rate obtained in the interviews (211 syll/min) was the same as the highest rate in the descriptions. Further analysis confirmed the difference between interviews and descriptions: a phonation-time ratio of 85 % in the former task and 59 % in the latter. This need to pause in the description of cartoons (speakers spent almost half of their speaking time being silent) is a good reflection of the cognitive and linguistic effort required; this involves, among other things, the visual decoding and comprehension of the pictures and the linguistic encoding of the oral description.

The slower speaking rate in descriptions can be accounted for in part by a slower articulation rate: 4.3 syll/sec (median) as compared to 5.2 syll/sec in the interview situation. Articulation rate was not correlated with speaking rate in the descriptions ($r = 0.05$) whereas the opposite was true in the interviews ($r = 0.78$). This is due to the fact that the lower the P.T.R., the more the pause time becomes an important factor in the computation of the speaking rate (as is the case in the descriptions). On the other hand, when the P.T.R. is very high (as in the interviews), then the articulation rate becomes the predominant factor in calculating the speaking rate.

A second variable which accounted for the slower speaking rate in descriptions was the length of the runs. These were half the length of those in interviews (6.5 syll/run as opposed to 12 syll/run). And a third variable which slowed down the speaking rate was the length of the pauses; they were more than twice as long in descriptions than in interviews (1.12 sec (median) and 0.48 sec respectively).

Thus, each of the three component variables of speaking rate played a role in the reduction of global rate, but they did so to varying degrees. The articulation rate was not as important a factor as the length of the runs and the duration of pauses. It is interesting to note that when readers slow down, they change the values of the component variables in similar ways. However, in this case, the pauses are not lengthened to the same extent (Grosjean, 1972; Grosjean and Collins, 1979). Thus, a slower reading rate is obtained by reducing the articulation rate but mainly by shortening the runs (i.e., inserting more pauses). The fact that speakers describing cartoons also lengthen their pauses clearly reflects the complexity of the task at hand – not only do they need to slow down their articulation rate and reduce the length of the runs (as do readers) but they also need to lengthen their pauses in order to accomplish the various cognitive and linguistic operations that are involved in description. We should note at this point that Goldman-Eisler's suggestion that conversational speech and description require a similar level of cognitive effort is not confirmed by this study. However, the term 'conversational speech' can describe a variety of speech productions which range from extremely fluent speech (as in the case of our interviews) to very hesitant speech. The conversational speech analyzed by Goldman-Eisler may have been of this latter type.

A syntactic analysis of the pauses in descriptions and interviews revealed that they occur in very similar locations. For example, 62 % of pauses in the former task and 61 % in interviews occur at the end of clauses and sentences. It is only when one examines the syntactic boundaries more closely that one notices a few differences; descriptions have more pauses after simple sentences (+ 9 %), less pauses after subordinate clauses (- 6 %) and after adverbial complements (- 4 %). These differences are due to the simpler sentence construction used in the descriptions: a greater number of simple active declarative sentences, less subordinate clauses, etc.

A comparison of hesitation phenomena in the two tasks showed a very similar rank ordering of the different types of pauses (filled pauses, drawls, repeats and false starts) but a doubling in number in the descriptions. It should be noted however that the mean length of unfilled pauses was found to be practically identical in the two tasks: 0.44 sec in the descriptions and 0.52 sec in the interviews. Although speakers could not lengthen their filled pauses in the descriptions (probably for articulatory reasons) they made up for them by inserting more drawls, repeats and false starts.

In summary, descriptions, when compared with interviews, are produced more slowly (due to a slower articulation rate but especially to more and longer pauses) and with many more hesitation pauses. These are of the same type in the two tasks, however, and they occur in very similar syntactic positions.

Within-language research on temporal variables needs to be pursued in order to ascertain to what extent these variables are affected when speakers are involved in such tasks as reports, discussions, monologues, etc. In addition, such factors as age, sex, social-economic background and language situation should be studied. Research of this type (see, for example, Hawkins, 1973; Kowal, O'Connell and Sabin, 1975; Duez, 1976) will allow us ultimately to isolate those temporal variables that remain relatively constant across linguistic tasks and speaker type and those that are influenced by linguistic, psychological and sociological factors.

3. Temporal Variables Between Languages: English and French

Literature on temporal variables is quite extensive but most studies are only concerned with one language, English. It is only in recent years that researchers have been interested in comparing temporal variables across languages with the aim of uncovering those aspects that are language specific and those that are common to language in general.

Grosjean and Deschamps (1973; 1975) were interested in comparing English and French. In the first study, they contrasted the results they obtained from cartoon descriptions with those published by Goldman-Eisler (1968) and Quinting (1971) for the same task in English. The speaking rates were very similar in the two languages (118 and 111 words/min in French and English respectively) and so were the P.T.R.'s (59 % and 56 % respectively). In addition, the articulation rates were identical (3.4 and 3.5 words/sec). Although the pause time was the same in English and French, its organization differed in the two languages: runs were longer in French (6.22 words/pause as compared to 4.67 words/pause in English) and pauses were shorter in English (0.86 sec as opposed to 1.12 sec in French).

So as to investigate further the similarities and differences between English and French, Grosjean and Deschamps (1975) undertook an extensive study of radio interviews in the two languages. Thirty interviews presented by the B.B.C. were compared to an equal number of interviews recorded from the O.R.T.F. (Grosjean and Deschamps, 1972). In the following review of this contrastive study we will first summarize the similarities that were found between the two languages and then concentrate on the two main differences that were uncovered.

The speakers of the two languages again presented very similar speaking rates and P.T.R.'s (264 syll/min and 85 % in French and 255 syll/min and 83 % in English; these differences were not significant). In addition, the articulation rates were once again not significantly different in the two languages: 5.21 syll/sec in French and 5.0 syll/sec in English). The length of silent pauses was identical in the two languages at the end of sentences (a mean of 0.48 sec in English and 0.50 in French) and within sentences (0.42 sec and 0.40 sec respectively), and the two sets of interviews were characterized by an identical number of hesitations (one every 24 syllables in French and one every 22 syllables in English). Finally, an identical percentage of filled pauses within and at the end of sentences was found, and the two languages presented identical patterns within each hesitation type: drawls were mainly made up of one-syllable grammatical words; two thirds of the repeats involved grammatical words and a bit more than half of the false starts in the two languages were corrected.

This list of similarities is quite impressive and one can only wonder how much of it is due to the fact that both languages belong to the Indo-European group and how much to the similar linguistic and cognitive operations involved in an interview situation (an identical study comparing two very different languages would help answer this question). Two interesting differences were found however in our comparison of English and French: the pause time (or P.T.R.), although identical in the two sets of interviews, was organized differently in the two languages (thus confirming the difference found by Grosjean and Deschamps (1973)), and filled pauses and drawls did not share the same importance in English and French.

First, pauses were once again shorter in English (0.44 sec as compared to 0.48 sec in French) and runs were again longer in French (12 syll/run as compared to 9.5 syll/run in English). The reason for the longer runs in French is difficult to isolate. An examination of the data enabled us to reject three possibilities: speakers of English need to breathe more often than speakers of French; speakers of English need to insert more unfilled hesitation pauses and English interviews contain shorter words than French interviews. We retained two possible reasons. The first concerns the fact that English often appears to be more concise than French. For example, English uses prepositions when a verb is needed in French (e.g. He came for his mail —> Il est venu prendre son courrier); emphatic stress in English must be expressed verbally in French (e.g. *Do* be careful —> surtout faites bien attention); the possessive case and compound nouns are expressed differently in the two languages (e.g. the government's income policy —> la politique des revenus du gouvernement) and certain individual lexical items in English are expressed in lengthier forms in French (e.g. a shipyard —> un chantier de construction naval). This conciseness of English can be seen in bilingual books where one page of French corresponds to 3/4 of a page in English. Whether this reason alone explains the shorter runs in English (and hence the shorter pauses) needs to be investigated further.

A second, and maybe more important, reason for the different organization of the pause time in the two languages is the presence of many more pauses in the VP in English than in French. If we compare a text in French containing 100 pauses and an English text of the same length, 75 % of the extra pauses in English, i.e. 19 pauses (the ratio of the number of pauses in English to the number of pauses in French is 1.19) are found inside sentences and especially inside the VP. It would appear that English simply has an additional pause location of importance (23 % of all pauses in English were located inside the VP as compared to 9 % only in French) and this results in a reduction in the length of the runs in the language. As more pauses occur in English, the pauses do not have to be as long and thus the two languages share identical pause times (15.5 % of the total speaking time in French and 16.8 % in English; the small difference is not significant). We can postulate from this that spoken utterances of equal length in various oral languages will probably have identical pause time ratios (when such variables as age, sex, linguistic task, situation etc., are controlled) but that the syntactic and morphological structure of each language will account for the distribution of the pause time.

A second difference that was uncovered in the comparative analysis of English and French concerns filled pauses and drawls. The grand total of filled pauses *and* drawls (the two made up the category 'pauses sonores') was identical in the two languages (69 % of all secondary variables in French and 71 % in English), but speakers of French produced almost as many drawls as filled pauses (30 % and 39 % respectively) whereas English speakers inserted many more filled pauses than drawls (53 % and 18 % respectively).

This can be explained by the fact that French is largely an open syllable language and speakers are free to lengthen mono- and polysyllabic words when they feel the need to hesitate, whereas English is a closed syllable language and speakers must therefore use filled pauses in preference to drawls. From this we can postulate that drawls and filled pauses probably have the same hesitation function and that the phonotactic configuration of the different oral languages will lead speakers to use one form of hesitation over another. We should note that this compensation effect will not extend to the other secondary variables (repeats and false starts) as these hesitation phenomena probably play a different psycholinguistic role. (The exact role of unfilled hesitation pauses, filled pauses and drawls, repeats and false starts and the reason for choosing one over the other still need to be explained adequately).

Comparative studies such as these need to be extended to other linguistic tasks and especially to other languages. This would allow one to verify, among other things, the two compensation effects found by Grosjean and Deschamps (1975): equal pause time across languages but a differing organization of this time within each language or language group, and an equal number of filled pauses-drawls but again a differing distribution of these two pauses depending on the phonotactic configuration of the languages.

4. *Temporal Variables Between Language Modalities: English and American Sign Language*

Cross-linguistic research on temporal variables is being pursued actively but most researchers have so far limited their comparisons to oral languages. It is only by extending this comparison to languages in another modality — the manual-visual modality — that truly universal factors will be uncovered. Such languages are the sign languages of the deaf. One of these languages, the sign language used by deaf communities in the United States, known as American Sign Language (ASL), has recently become the object of systematic research by linguists and psychologists. They have shown that this language, which should be distinguished from fingerspelling — a visual representation of the English alphabet — is a systematic natural form of symbolical communication among a stable community of users. It has the degree of regularity and structure required of a fully developed language and is not some form of English on the hands. ASL is a different language with different structural principles. For example, a sign in ASL is composed of at least four distinct parameters: shape of the hand, location of the hand, orientation of the palm and movement of the hand. To illustrate this, the sign for the concept GIRL is made with the hand in a fist, the thumb tip brushing down the lower cheek.

In the following section we will review our work on the temporal variables in ASL and English and will attempt to isolate and account for those aspects of language processing which are common to both modalities and those on which they differ.

In a first study (Grosjean, 1977), we examined the perception of rate by listeners and observers (extraphonic rate) and by signers and speakers (autophonic rate). We found that listeners (for speech) and observers (for sign) perceived changes in rate very differently. When a signer or speaker doubled his rate, an observer would perceive a threefold increase in the signer's rate whereas a listener would perceive almost a fourfold increase in the speaker's change of rate. We ascribed this difference in perception of rate to the different perceptual modalities involved — auditory on the one hand and visual on the other.

The divergence we found in the listener's and observer's perception of rate led us to ask the following question: When the change of rate is under the control of the speaker and signer, will their perception of their own change of rate also be different? In the same study (Grosjean, 1977), we found that speakers and signers covered the same range of rate when progressing from a slow to a fast rate (signers covered a 2.6 : 1 range and speakers a 2.7 : 1 range). This means that both signers and speakers perceived changes of their own rate in a similar fashion: when a speaker or a signer doubles his rate, he perceives about a sixfold increase. This result suggests that a mechanism common to both speakers and signers, possibly involving proprioception, mediates both types of rate judgment.

This finding led us to investigate the manner in which signers and speakers modify their production rate (Grosjean, 1979). We found that both signers and speakers modify the articulation time and pause time in their productions when asked to speed up or slow down, but that the relative importance of these two variables will differ in the two modalities: signers will alter their rate by mainly changing the time they spend articulating whereas speakers primarily modify the pause time (by inserting or extracting pauses) and hardly alter their articulation time. These different strategies were accounted for by the role of breathing in speech and sign. As signing is an activity that is independent of breathing (Grosjean, 1979), signers will alter their rate by mainly changing the time they spend articulating whereas speakers, especially at slow rate, are compelled by breathing demands to put numerous pauses into their speech and must therefore use this approach to alter their rate. At slow rate, speakers only have enough air reserve to articulate a few words. When this reserve is used up, they must stop articulating and inhale so as to be able to continue articulating.

We also examined the factors which influence the articulation time of signs and words and those that affect the frequency, relative duration and location of pauses in the two languages. Klatt (1976) lists a number of factors that influence the durational structure of units in speech: the psychological and physical state of the speaker, speaking rate, position of the element within a paragraph, emphasis and semantic novelty, phrase structure lengthening, word-final lengthening, inherent phonological duration of a segment, effect of linguistic stress, effect of postvocalic consonant and segmental interactions (e.g. consonant clusters). Evidence was found that a number of these factors, restated in terms of a visual-manual language as necessary, also influence the duration of signs. They were the inherent duration of signs, the signing rate, the semantic novelty of a sign and the phrase structure lengthening in a sign sentence. For example, as rate increased, the duration of signs decreased. At a rate of 176 signs per minute (spm) the mean duration of signs was 0.16 sec with a range extending from 0.07 sec (for the sign REALLY) to 0.33 sec (CHAIRS). And as signing rate was decreased, signs were increased in duration. The mean duration of signs at 35 spm was 0.69 sec with values ranging from 0.28 sec (HARD) to 1.90 sec (LONG-TIME-AGO). Also, the semantic novelty of a sign affects its duration. Signs which occur twice in the same syntactic position are on average 10 % shorter on the second occurrence. And signs like words are influenced by phrase structure lengthening. It was found that signs at the end of sentences are about 12 % longer than within sentences.

These findings (signers and speakers cover an equal range of rate when asked to speed up or slow down; they do this by varying the articulation time and the pause time (admittingly to a varying degree); the duration of both signs and words are influenced by a number of common factors) led Grosjean (1978) to postulate some common mechanism that mediates to some extent at least both sign and speech production. This premise was further strengthened when we examined the distribution of pauses in sign and speech and the hierarchical organization of the speaker's and signer's output.

Grosjean and Lane (1977) found that in sign, as in speech, to a hierarchy of pause frequency and duration corresponds a hierarchy of constituents. The durations of pauses in ASL indicate not only the breaks between simple sentences and between conjoined sentences (pauses between conjoined sentences were systematically shorter than between simple sentences) but also the boundaries between and within major constituents of these sentences. What is interesting is that when the data is not averaged across sentences, a number of mismatches were found between the constituent structure of the sentence and the pause durations. This fact was first uncovered in a study on speech (Grosjean, Grosjean and Lane, 1979) where it was shown that the surface structure of a sentence is a good predictor of the pause data only when sentences and constituents are of equal length. The mismatches that occurred between pause duration and the structural complexity index were due primarily to subjects' concurrent tendency to distribute pauses so as to bisect the sentences and constituents. When constituents are of unequal length, Ss will attempt to displace the pause to a point midway between the beginning of the first constituent (for example, an NP) and the end of the second constituent (for example, a VP), if at that point there occurs a syntactic boundary important enough. It would seem that a compromise takes place between this bisection tendency and the linguistic structure of the sentence. Grosjean, Grosjean and Lane (1979) developed a model to assign to each word boundary in a sentence a predicted share of the total pause duration in light of its structural complexity and its distance from the bisection point. The model accounted for 72 % of the total variance in pause time as compared to 56 % accounted for by a linguistic structure complexity index alone.

The question for sign now became: Does a formal model of syntactic structure alone account for the experimental data obtained from pausing (Grosjean and Lane, 1977) or does the signer, like the speaker, need to make a compromise between two, sometimes conflicting demands: the need to respect the linguistic structure of the sentence and the need to balance the length of the constituents in the output. If this were the case, it would greatly strengthen our premise that some common mechanism, influenced by a number of identical factors, mediates sign and speech production. We found that our model of performance pause structure in speech (Grosjean, Grosjean and Lane, 1979) predicted the Grosjean and Lane (1977) pause values in sign better than the ASL linguistic structure by itself ($r = 0.85$ as opposed to $r = 0.78$) and present experimental research is confirming this finding. Performance structures would therefore be founded in the decoding and encoding of language (be it visual or oral) and not in the properties of any particular communication modality.

To conclude, Grosjean (1978) proposed that although speech and sign differ on many aspects, they probably share some common production mechanism. This mechanism is influenced by such factors as the rate of output, the semantic novelty of words and signs, the syntactic structure of the sentences and the tendency for the system to produce constituents of equal length. This common mechanism needs to be investigated further and inserted into a global model of language production and perception in which aspects common to sign and spoken languages and aspects specific to each modality would be clearly identified. This should be one of the goals of modern psycholinguistic research.

5. *Future Perspectives*

Cross-linguistic studies of temporal variables will become more numerous in the years to come and it is our hope that researchers will keep in mind the following points:

a) Different languages, belonging to various language groups and to both the spoken and sign modalities, should be compared in well delimited tasks. Research so far has concentrated on too few languages (often belonging to the same language group) and the task given to speakers has not always been well defined. This extensive and controlled research will help us uncover those aspects of temporal variables that are specific to individual languages, to language groups and to language modality, and those that are common to language in general.

b) Research on temporal variables should not only study global phenomena (for example, the articulation rate of a passage or the number of pauses it contains) but should narrow in on certain specific questions such as: how are temporal variables used in the disambiguation of sentences across languages? How do bilinguals deal with the compensatory effects uncovered by Grosjean and Deschamps (1975)? Are temporal variables used in the same way to mark embedded clauses, emphatic stress, fronting, etc. in languages belonging to different language groups?

c) Studies on temporal variables should deal as much with perception as with production. Much of the existing work has been concerned with production but is it not as important to uncover how listeners process temporal variables? Do all languages use the same temporal cues to signal syntactic breaks or to disambiguate sentences? Are unfilled pauses really needed by the listener in his segmentation of the speech stream (as seems to be the case for non-native speakers of a language (Grosjean, 1972))? Cross-linguistic perceptual studies on temporal variables should be encouraged in the years to come.

d) Other prosodic variables should be involved in this research. Many studies on temporal variables have been concerned with a limited set of variables. But when a speaker inserts a silent pause in an utterance, it has important repercussions not only on the speaking rate and the mean frequency and duration of pauses, but also on the fundamental frequency and the amplitude of the signal, the lengthening of the syllables preceding the pause, etc. Likewise, the insertion of a filled pause and the presence of a false start should not be studied independently of other speech errors such as slips of the tongue, spoonerisms, etc. (Fromkin, 1971, 1973; Garrett, 1975). The interdependence of temporal variables and other prosodic variables (Martin (1970) reports the perceptual presence of pauses when no silence occurred in the speech stream) and of hesitation phenomena with speech errors is complex and needs to be studied carefully by researchers who are ready to go beyond their own domain of research.

e) Finally, research on temporal variables should be integrated to ongoing research in linguistics and psycholinguistics. Studying temporal variables for their own sake is important but it is even more valuable to integrate the results obtained into a model (or models) of production, perception and language acquisition (see Goldman-Eisler (1968) for an example of this). Many studies on temporal variables have not had the impact they deserve because the authors did not make enough effort to integrate their findings with existing models. It is our hope that future research will help to remedy this.

REFERENCES

BARIK, H. 1977. Cross-Linguistic Study of Temporal Characteristics of Different Types of Speech Material. *Language and Speech.* 20, 116-126.

BLANKENSHIP, J. and C. Kay. 1964. Hesitation Phenomena in English Speech: A Study in Distribution. *Word.* 20, 360-372.

DUEZ, D. 1976. Etude du débit et des pauses d'un discours politique. *Bulletin de l'Institut de Phonétique de Grenoble.* 5, 39-53.

FROMKIN, V.A. 1971. The Non-Anomalous Nature of Anomalous Utterances. *Language.* 47, 27-52.

FROMKIN, V.A. 1973. Slips of the Tongue. *Scientific American.* 229, 109-117.

GARRETT, M.F. 1975. The Analysis of Sentence Production. In: G.H. Bower (ed.). *The Psychology of Learning and Motivation.* Vol. 9. New York: Academic Press, 133-177.

GOLDMAN-EISLER, F. 1968. *Psycholinguistics: Experiments in Spontaneous Speech.* London, New York: Academic Press.

GROSJEAN, F. 1972. *Le rôle joué par trois variables temporelles dans la compréhension orale de l'anglais étudié comme seconde langue et perception de la vitesse de lecture par des lecteurs et des auditeurs.* Doctoral Dissertation. University of Paris VII.

GROSJEAN, F. 1977. The Perception of Rate in Spoken and Sign Languages. *Perception and Psychophysics.* 22, 408-413.

GROSIEAN, F. 1978. Cross-Linguistic Research in the Perception and Production of English and American Sign Language. Paper presented at the Second National Symposium on Sign Language Research and Teaching. Coronado, California.

GROSJEAN, F. 1979. A Study of Timing in a Manual and a Spoken Language: American Sign Language and English. *Journal of Psycholinguistic Research.* 8, 379-405.

GROSJEAN, F. and M. Collins. 1979 (in press). Breathing, Pausing and Reading. *Phonetica.* 36, 98-114.

GROSJEAN, F. and A. Deschamps. 1972. Analyse des variables temporelles du français spontané. *Phonetica.* 26, 129-156.

GROSJEAN, F. and A. Deschamps. 1973. Analyse des variables temporelles du français spontané. II. Comparaison du français oral dans la description avec l'anglais (description) et avec le français (interview radiophonique). *Phonetica.* 28, 191-226.

GROSJEAN, F. and A. Deschamps. 1975. Analyse contrastive des variables temporelles de l'anglais et du français: vitesse de parole et variables composantes, phénomènes d'hésitation. *Phonetica*. 31, 144-184.

GROSJEAN, F., F. Grosjean and H. Lane. 1979 (in press). The Patterns of Silence: Performance Structures in Sentence Production. *Cognitive Psychology*. 11, 58-81.

GROSJEAN, F. and H. Lane. 1977. Pauses and Syntax in American Sign Language. *Cognition*. 5, 101-117.

HAWKINS, P. 1973. The Influence of Sex, Social Class and Pause Location in the Hesitation Phenomena of Seven-Year-Old Children. In: B. Bernstein (ed.). *Class, Codes and Control*. Vol. 2. London: Routledge and Kegan Paul.

KELLY, J. and M. Steer. 1949. Revised Concept of Rate. *Journal of Speech and Hearing Disorders*. 14, 222-226.

KLATT, D. 1976. Linguistic Uses of Segmental Duration in English: Acoustic and Perceptual Evidence. *Journal of the Acoustical Society of America*. 59, 1208-1221.

KOWAL, S., D. O'Connell and E. Sabin. 1975. Development of Temporal Patterning and Vocal Hesitations in Spontaneous Narratives. *Journal of Psycholinguistic Research*. 4, 195-207.

LUCCI, V. 1973. Etude phonostylistique du rythme et de la variabilité de la longueur en français parlé et français lu. *Bulletin de l'Institut de Phonétique de Grenoble*. 2, 139-161.

LUCCI, V. 1974. Rythme et longueur du message parlé. La conversation. *Bulletin de l'Institut de Phonétique de Grenoble*. 3, 139-152.

MACLAY, H. and C. Osgood. 1959. Hesitation Phenomena in Spontaneous English Speech. *Word*. 15, 19-44.

MARTIN, J. 1970. On Judging Pauses in Spontaneous Speech. *Journal of Verbal Learning and Verbal Behavior*. 9, 75-78.

O'CONNELL, D. and S. Kowal. 1972. Cross-Linguistic Pause and Rate Phenomena in Adults and Adolescents. *Journal of Psycholinguistic Research*. 1, 155-164.

QUINTING, G. 1971. *Hesitation Phenomena in Adult Aphasic and Normal Speech*. The Hague, Paris: Mouton.

SAINT-BONNET, M. et J. Boë. 1977. Les pauses et les groupes rythmiques: leur durée et distribution en fonction de la vitesse d'élocution. *Compte Rendu des VIIIe Journées d'Etude sur la Parole*. Aix en Provence.

THE ANALYSIS OF CROSS-LANGUAGE COMMUNICATION: PROLEGOMENA TO THE THEORY AND METHODOLOGY

Kari Sajavaara and Jaakko Lehtonen
University of Jyväskylä, Finland

Introduction

After three decades of contrastive linguistics it is clear that what can be termed traditional contrastive analysis has failed to meet the highly practical objectives which were set for it. A great number of books and papers have been published on language contrasts but the amount of CA that can be called applied remains insignificant. More and more people accept, therefore, the criticism directed against the usefulness of contrastive analysis, a view that has been strengthened by the influence of recent American research on second language acquisition.

The traditional methodology of contrastive analysis centres on the problem of deviance in the structural programming of the target language, and it mostly fails to see the non-native speaker's speech performance in the wider framework of a bilingual speaker's attempt at communicative success. At the early stages, most contrastive analysis concentrated on rather abstract structural topics. More recently, traditional contrastive analysis has sometimes been supplemented by studies dealing with what has been labelled as contrastive textlinguistics or contrastive discourse analysis. In such studies, the analysis has been expanded to cover certain categories lying beyond the sentence boundary but the basically structure-centred orientation usually prevails.

The main target of pedagogical CA should however be the phenomena which are characteristic of a 'bilingual' speaker using L2 as compared to his use of L1, and the native speaker's reaction to such a speech performance. Contrastive analysis is a typical branch of applied linguistics. This does not mean that CA is an activity whose *only* aim is to apply linguistics for practical purposes outside the scope of pure linguistics. It cannot rely on linguistics alone; it works with similarities and differences in human verbal and non-verbal codes and with the clash of the two codes in the language-behaviour of a foreign language student. In view of what is today expected of CA, it will have to absorb both theoretical perspectives and practical methodology from various branches of the disciplines which deal with language and speech or human behaviour in general. This definition of contrastive analysis implies that CA is no longer a special branch of pure linguistics only. The theory and methodology of linguistics used must inevitably be supplemented by those of such disciplines as sociology, psychology, neurology, and applied mathematics, as concerns the analysis and description of pragmatic patterning, cognitive mechanisms, perception, and information-processing systems in man. The expanded objectives of contrastive analysis are, to a large extent, parallel to the goals of the modern communication-sciences, which aim at the examination of various aspects of human communication.

Traditional Contrastive Analysis

Ever since the term 'contrastive linguistics' was adopted to describe a certain type of comparison between two or more languages, such analysis has been subjected to great expectations and severe criticism (see Sajavaara, 1977). Recent literature gives the impression that contrastive linguistics has been in a state of serious crisis since the early 1960s. This crisis is mainly due to a contradiction between the theoretical basis of CA and its objectives and mainly results from the past history of CA.

The early stages of CA are linked with American structuralism. In the United States, the culmination was the publication in 1962-1965 of the Contrastive Structure series and the 1968 Georgetown Round Table meeting. At the Georgetown Round Table a deep note of criticism was sounded and error analysis was introduced as a 'contestant'; American contrastive linguistics practically died out as a result of this criticism. The interest was however revived in Europe, and a number of projects were launched in the mid-sixties with pedagogical applications as one of their major objectives; several new projects were started in the 1970s, all of them applying eclectic methodology and aiming at practical objectives.

The reasons for the failure of traditional contrastive linguistics are many. Structuralists emphasized the importance of the internal structure of each individual language, and therefore they were not interested in similarities and differences between languages. This meant that the starting-point for CA was not the best possible.

Descriptions of individual languages necessary for CA have generally reflected the development of linguistic theory, which has been another source of concern for traditional contrastive linguistics. The best model for theoretical CA is the one that gives the most comprehensive explanation of linguistic phenomena (see Fisiak et al., 1978), but such a model is not necessarily the best for applied contrastive purposes. No generally accepted model is available today, and descriptions of any two languages according to one model, which is one of the prerequisites of traditional CA, are rare. The expansion of purely grammatical analysis beyond the sentence offers no major breakthrough for CA. Moreover, the independence of the descriptions of the two languages has been illusory. The major grammatical models have been created in close adherence to descriptions of certain individual languages: describing other languages by these models means contrasting these languages with the original model language.

Contradictions in contrastive methodology have been another source of criticism. Translation equivalence as established by a bilingual informant has generally been considered a satisfactory starting-point, but it is not unambiguous as a theoretical concept (see Krzeszowski, 1974). Moreover, no method is available for the specification of the surface categories which correspond to deeper semantic and conceptual ones. This is one of the major reasons why contrastive analyses tend to result in parallel descriptions. The theory of transfer has played an important part in error analysis and applied CA. Negative transfer has been regarded as one of the primary sources of erroneous forms in the learner's language, but the problem is the same as with equivalence: it has been difficult to establish the units that are transferred, and the level at which the transfer takes place.

The abstractness of CA has also been a fruitful source of criticism. Traditional CA has been abstract because it has been far removed from the reality of the language learner. Moreover, purely theoretical CA has been performed for the purposes of language teaching, and many contrastive descriptions have been derived from models of competence without any link to the performance of individual users of the languages contrasted.

Traditional CA implies a static view of interlingual contrasts. The source and target languages are regarded as equal for the learner, and the learner's position in relation to the target language is considered stable. Language learning is not seen as a process, and the language contrasts established are contrasts between final products and not between intermediate stages before the final product is reached. Little attention has, moreover, been paid to the shifting of the roles of the speaker and hearer in a communicative situation.

Most of the criticism has centred on the inability of CA to meet its non-theoretical objectives. It is evident that the basic idea behind the contrasting of languages is not wrong, because enough evidence is available of the existence of foreign accents in the speech of non-native speakers. The source of the problem must be sought in the insufficiency of linguistic parameters to solve problems which are not linguistic alone.

Error analysis has often been offered as a replacement for CA or as a primary level of analysis to which CA is to be subordinate. Applied CA and EA are, however, methods which have one and the same target: the problems of the learner's language. In interlanguage studies, a static view is supposed to give way to the observation of the language learning processes. CA, EA and interlanguage studies are integral parts of research into the problems of learning strategies. In this work, the emphasis should lie on the learner's language as a whole.

As the above discussion of traditional contrastive linguistics shows, the theory and methodology of CA have remained undeveloped. CA has usually had a purely linguistic starting-point, and the interrelationship between CA and the theories of language acquisition and language learning has been vague. Only occasionally has an attempt been made to connect the two (the Kiel project (see Wode, 1978) and the Copenhagen PIF project are outstanding exceptions). Theoretical linguistic analysis can never solve problems which are not linguistic alone but which require multidisciplinary approaches. Several writers, eg. Fisiak in several papers (eg., 1973), have pointed out that it is necessary to make a distinction between theoretical and applied contrastive studies and that theoretical contrastive linguistics is a branch of theoretical linguistics. Theoretical linguistics, for its part, has undergone a hectic period of upheaval during the past twenty years. Traditional and early structural views gave way to various generative approaches but today, instead of having a fairly universal frame of reference, we are in a situation in which it is impossible to tell what the next stage will be. What is beneficial, however, for CA in recent developments in the fact that linguistics has widened beyond traditional code-centred approaches. Pure analysis of grammatical competence has been replaced by research in which man's social and communicative competence are given their proper share and where language and the use of language are seen as dynamic processes.

A communicative approach to cross-language phenomena calls attention to the language behaviour of the human being in various interactional situations, to his ability to use different channels of communication to convey messages and intentions, and to his ability to understand and interpret messages transmitted by the other interactants in communication. In such research, the linguistic code and the grammatical structures embedded in the code have an instrumental function only. It is true that the final product of language learning is expected to be a native speaker's proficiency in the language concerned, and the proper use of language structures is obviously an integral part of such proficiency, but in the processes that lead to the definitive proficiency, the structures of the linguistic code are subordinated to various communicative strategies. Therefore, the research dealing with the morpheme acquisition sequence, for instance, will be able to give only partial answers unless it is supplemented by research that posits the morphemes in a communicative framework.

It is quite understandable that the linguist's attention has been primarily focussed on the linguistic code, but this does not legitimize the assumption, so common among linguists, that the categories and phenomena abstracted for a linguistic analysis of the code are constructs that can be transferred as such to the analysis of speech perception and speech processing (cf. Clark and Clark, 1977: 190). This is strongly emphasized by Ladefoged (1977 : 410): " ... although linguists may be able to define units all the way up from bundles of features to prosodies of sentences, it is by no means clear what use is made of these units in communicative acts."

Besides the shift away from the predominance of purely linguistic factors to communicative ones CA must also undergo another shift. Since learning L2 means an expansion of communicative competence into the area of another code, the learner's role requires much greater attention than has been directed to it so far. A large body of literature which has accumulated in the last few years purports to show that people learn second languages in the same way as they learn their first languages, and learners of English, whether they approach English as an L1 or L2, go through more or less the same processes irrespective of their mother tongue (see, e.g., Hatch, 1977 and Hakuta and Cancino, 1977). This research is, however, concerned with learners acquiring a second language in natural settings. Recent research on language acquisition presents a uniform picture of the acquisition sequence of certain English morphemes (see Krashen, 1977). However, children do not acquire morphemes but a means to communicate their needs. Successful language acquirers are more concerned with communication than with form (see eg., Fillmore, 1976), and parents pay attention to their children's messages and not to their grammar (see Snow and Ferguson (eds.), 1977; Waterson and Snow (eds.), 1978). The input/intake system is of primary importance for acquisition. Morpheme sequence studies must be supplemented by research based on discourse entities and on various communicative and other functions of linguistic elements (see also Frith, 1976: 120-121). This kind of detailed research may reveal new relationships between L1 and L2.

In some recent work on how people acquire second languages, a difference has been made between conscious language learning (memorization of rules) and unconscious acquisition, which results from mere exposure to the target language (similarly to first languages). Krashen's (1978) Monitor Model ist the most developed attempt to synthesize the information available about the two processes. According to Krashen, speech performance is always initiated by means of the acquired system and the learned system is available as a monitor for editing the output. In acquisition-poor environments a speaker must rely on his L1 competence as a performance initiator. The initial L1 string is then 'translated' into an L2 string, whose grammaticality and acceptability depend on the availability of 'rules' and on the nature of the constraints present. As a result of optimal acquisition the L2 string is initiated and processed on the basis of the acquired L2 system without the interference of Krashen's Monitor. In this way we have two extremes: at one end we have total acquisition, which results in native-like performance without a trace of L1 influence, and at the other end we have a language system in L2 which is based entirely on explicit memorization of rules, which is sufficient for the production of acceptable L2 strings under favourable circumstances. Most L2 speakers are located somewhere between the two extremes; at least occasionally, they have to rely on the L1 systems for speech reception and production. This is the case when the L2 unit has not been acquired and the monitor fails to give the right answer. There may be no rules, the rules have not been 'taught', the rules may be wrong, or the speaker may apply 'wrong' rules belonging to either L1 or L2 (or a third language). If the acquisition/learning dichotomy proposed by Krashen is correct, L1 influence on L2 surface strings may be due to the fact that (1) the string has been initiated by the acquired L1 system and the monitor has not been able to correct the string, (2) the monitor lacks the correct 'rule' and an L1 rule is used as a repair, or (3) strings originally initated with correct L2 acquired systems are mutilated by the learned system (see Sajavaara 1978b).

The L1 and L2 acquired and learned systems are closely interlinked, and both of the systems are referred to several times during speech production, which may result in highly variable performance by the same speakers in different situations. This implies that interference from L1 is a complex system of interrelationships and that the research on language transfer has had far too simple a starting-point. We have only the final product, the surface string, and the processes that have led to it remain obscure. We need methods to study the stages before the actual utterance. We can start, for instance, by replicating Mahl's (1972) experiments with prevented audiomonitoring and delayed feedback. On the basis of Labov's (1970) findings it could be hypothesized that prevented audiomonitoring would result in the increase of L1 influence in the speech of nonnative speakers whose acquisition level is low. Other methods are needed in which the functioning of the 'monitor' could be observed. The preliminary experiments with Finnish speakers of English using feedback and prevented audiomonitoring which were carried out by the Finnish-English Contrastive Project gave conflicting results and more material is needed before any conclusions can be drawn.

Expanding the Framework

A review of the history of contrastive linguistics implies clearly that, irrespective of the model used, mere contrasting of structural categories or sets of categories in two or more languages is insufficient for pedagogical purposes. The fundamental role of a human language is to function as a means of communication in human interaction, and it seems obvious that, in addition to the parallel descriptions of the grammatical structures, the differences and similarities in the processes which take place in the speaker and the listener during acts of communication will have to be mapped across languages. Contrastive analysis is expanded, in this way, to cover all the phenomena that are part of human behaviour in interactional settings. Particular emphasis should be put on parameters outside the linguistic code pure and proper:

> ... the so-called extralinguistic and nonverbal aspects of communication aren't mere window-dressing that accompany sentences optionally but a fundamental ingredient of the process by which people decode and encode messages. Many propositional and symbolic components of communicative interactions are not expressed by linguistic means but rather by way of conventionalized manual gestures, body movements, facial expressions, and prosodic elements beyond phonology. (Lamendella, 1977 : 158).

Language is used by individuals for definite purposes, which are related to the speaker's intentions in some specific time and environment. This implies that any elements that make part of an utterance or some other behavioural phenomenon are always situation-specific. Before it is feasible to carry out any 'contrastive' analysis of the linguistic codes, the linguistic codes will have to be located in their proper place in the speech communication processes across languages. For this we need contrastive analysis of similarities and differences in the processes of communication, in the rules of interaction, and in the use of various non-verbal means in communication between two sociocultural settings.

As was pointed out above, one of the crucial questions in contrastive analysis has been the choice of the reference model: should CA be based on traditional structural, or generative grammar, and if so, which variety? Yet the practical choice is often eclectic: such grammatical theories are applied as they seem to give the best explanation in each problem. The alternative is to describe similarities and differences as well as interference phenomena between the two systems within the framework of a given theory of grammar irrespective of how practical or effective the theory concerned is in explaining various aspects in the complex of problems.

The choice of the reference model concerns not only the model to be used in the description of grammar but also the choice between a static and dynamic view of language or, in other words, the choice between a linguistic and psycholinguistic description, or between a structural and operational modelling of the communicative vehicle, i.e. language and the chain of speech (cf. Lehtonen, 1978c; see also Davis, 1978). The former (the structural model) aims at describing the abstracted and idealized structure of language, which, in the case of CA, means similarities and differences in the structures, or grammars, of two or more languages. Independently of the choice of the linguistic model, taxonomic or generative, the objective of such description is always the structure of the language instead of the actual processes (cf. e.g. Clark and Clark, 1977 : 190ff.).

The target of an operational model of language is not an abstracted static structure but language in action. In such a model, linguistic information is not processed in perception linearly or 'hierarchically' by proceeding step by step through the levels of grammar from a concrete level of representation to phonology and syntax, and further to abstract 'meaning'. Instead, the components of the system which exploit the hearer's phonological, syntactic, and pragmatic knowledge are supposed to work in perception simultaneously or in terms of a time-sharing system; active guesses are made and the probabilities for each hypothesis are weighed. This model implies that there are 'cues' for all levels of grammar in the flow of speech waves and the information involved is not present in the actual speech coded through phonology alone. Corresponding factors are also present in the process of message production, which, similarly, cannot be seen to be a chain of steps leading from higher linguistic levels through syntax and phonology to phonetics and actual physical speech. In perception, lexicon, syntax, and phonological structure all act as a set of constraints which reduce the number of probable 'guesses' in the process of linguistic identification of the acoustic speech input. The knowledge-driven process is in principle simultaneous with the input-driven analysis. In addition, there is a retroactive reworking effect, where the perception of a word or a sequence of words is changed afterwards on the basis of the subsequent context. These are all processes which are not normally accessible to consciousness. We only perceive the single final option, and not the preceding multitude of choices. Certain familiar phenomena of visual perception are similar to this process: in an ambiguous figure both interpretations are never seen simultaneously; the interpretation vacillates between the two (cf. Marslen-Wilson and Welsh, 1978).

As a result of the disintegration of the original Chomskyan borderline between competence and performance, linguistic competence is now seen as a part of the entire communicative behaviour of the human being. Grammatical competence has been replaced by communicative competence, which means the ability to communicate verbally and non-verbally in culturally restricted contexts and consists not only of grammatical competence but also of pragmatics. In communicative situations, the rules of the language game involve a variety of parameters which are related to linguistic, psycholinguistic, sociolinguistic, and sociopsychological phenomena. These parameters are constantly present when language is used, and our knowledge of how people use language will therefore have to be correlated with our knowledge of man's overall cognitive behaviour and perceptive capacities.

As was said before, traditional CA has been too abstract to specify the difficulties of a foreign language speaker in his attempt to use L2 for speech communication. The real contrast takes place in the learner and, therefore, the interaction between a Finnish speaker of English and a non-Finnish (not necessarily native) speaker of English, for instance, has to be studied as a whole. Attention must be paid to factors which make it possible for a Finn to understand messages in English, and to make himself understood. Attempts to delimit factors which characterize a Finnish speaker of English, for instance, in contrast to other non-native speakers are an essential part of such research. It presupposes a careful and detailed comparison of Finnish and native English speech and of communicative and language behaviour in both Finnish and English by the same Finnish informants.

Two approaches using the communicative perspective can be found in our pilot studies. One is the analysis of the linguistic and paralinguistic behaviour of speakers in communicative situations of a non-interactive nature, e.g. the reading of texts of varying complexity or the free delivery of speech during various types of narration tasks (for preliminary results see Sajavaara and Lehtonen, 1978b, and Lehtonen, 1978a). The other approach is the description of the communicative behaviour of native speakers and students — or schoolchildren — in different interactional situations. Particular emphasis has been laid on the problems connected with the non-native speaker's fluency as contrasted to that of the native speaker (see Sajavaara and Lehtonen, 1978b, and Sajavaara, 1977).

Contrastive Discourse Analysis

The concept of the speech chain is useful for the discussion of the problems in the analysis and physical description of the events in human speech and the relevant instrumental methods. Analyzing the speech chain means seeking the answer to questions such as how the messages are transmitted from one person to another or through what kind of transformations the message gets from the brain of the speaker to the brain of the hearer. Unfortunately, there are serious limitations to the capacity of the tests at present available for revealing the 'critical' points in the interlanguage speech channel, partly because we still lack an integrated picture of the mechanisms functioning in the transfer of information in normal language communication. The only method of testing speech perception which has been applied to CA has been identification tests based on minimal word pairs and other similar traditional methods of testing pronunciation. These methods are, however, so closely related to the taxonomic view of language that they are suitable for the testing of certain types of phonological contrasts only. There is, however, an indirect way of approaching the problems of foreign language speech perception: it is the analysis of the student's speech production. It can be hypothesized that deviations from the target in the production of the features which are known to function as cues for syntactic or semantic processing of utterances reflect corresponding difficulties in perceptual processing. Similarly, if some native-language features break through the pronunciation of the foreign language, the student may also be expected to apply the same cues when he is trying to process messages in the foreign language. The elements confused with each other may be quite unexpected. For instance, a Finn may meet difficulties in learning the fortis/lenis distinction of English consonants as a result of the long/short distinction of Finnish vowels; what a Finn regards as clarity in his pronunciation of English may be regarded as foreign accent and lack of fluency by a native speaker; errors in the pronunciation of certain sounds may be heard as changes in the stress pattern of the words, and so on. In most cases, traditional contrastive analysis has lacked power to give explanations of such cross-language influence.

Differences in the way in which two languages signal higher-level information such as morphological and syntactic patterns, lexical units or even textual features such as topicalization can also result in interference in speech communication. For instance, the process of how a lexical word is detected in English may be somewhat different from that used in Finnish as a consequence of linguistic differences between a primarily isolating language (English) and an agglutinating one (Finnish), although it is not possible to verify this hypothesis by the methods available at present. When the hypothesis is verified, however, we will have revealed an essential source of difficulty for a Finn in the comprehension of spoken English. This information may also be of considerable importance for attempts to find a way of teaching learners to overcome difficulties which are due to this higher-level interference phenomenon of phonetic processing.

There are a number of methods for the study of various peripheral phenomena of human speech (such as the movements of the organs of speech or speech acoustics), but we still lack methods for studying the phenomena in the central nervous system. The acoustic signal is the most easily accessible stage in the speech chain; it can be recorded on tape and analyzed by means of several acoustic research apparata. But when we move from research centred on the sound wave to research dealing with production or perception, the task becomes the more difficult the 'higher' the phenomenon which we want to study is in the speech chain. However, certain methods are within the reach of a contrastive linguist which are relevant in the analysis and testing of 'higher-level' linguistic problems such as sentence construction, conveyance of meaning through grammatical constructions and the speech chain, and the progress of discourse in real time. As was pointed out above, it is largely impossible for man to perceive physical speech events objectively. Therefore, one of the most essential applications of the instrumental methods for CA is the visualization of physical speech events. Two dimensions in particular are important for the analysis and description of linguistic structures larger than sound segments or individual words: these are the time axis of speech and the fluctuation of the fundamental frequency.

Figure 1 illustrates three fragments of discourse described in a form of an on/off signal on the real time-axis. The advantages of this kind of description as compared with traditional transcription are evident: In this method, we have access to the analysis of the distribution of speech performance in time, which is an integral element in the linguistic behaviour of man. This information is of special value in the analysis of discourse dynamics and tests in which information about reaction time, time of hesitation, location of pauses, etc., are needed. The present figure illustrates tracings from a four-channel apparatus designed for the analysis of discourse at the Phonetics Laboratory of the University of Jyväskylä. It makes possible the recording and analysis of simultaneous speaking turns (e.g., simultaneous starts, feedback moves of the listeners, and completions) as well as the chronemics of the discourse in general, which has so far been a parameter neglected in the analysis.

At the first stage of this work, small-group interaction in seminarlike settings and classroom interaction have been chosen as primary targets, but some research has also been carried out on casual conversations (Ventola, 1978). Several individual studies have been started, and three interactional situations have been examined in them: (1) situations involving dyadic communication, e.g. phone calls; (2) small-group interaction in which there are a maximum of four participants; and (3) classroom interaction. The materials from situations (2) and (3) are collected by means of videotaping.

Through the automatic processing of the material, a discourse map is produced where each participant's involvement is indicated by the shifts of the lines recorded. At the next stage the utterances of all participants are added to the map, and the verbal element can finally be supplemented by various kinesic and other

FIGURE 1

Three fragments of a discourse map consisting of the speaking turns and kinesics of three participants. Speaker A is a native speaker of English, and B and C are non-native (Finnish) speakers. The technique used makes it possible to study simultaneous speaking turns.

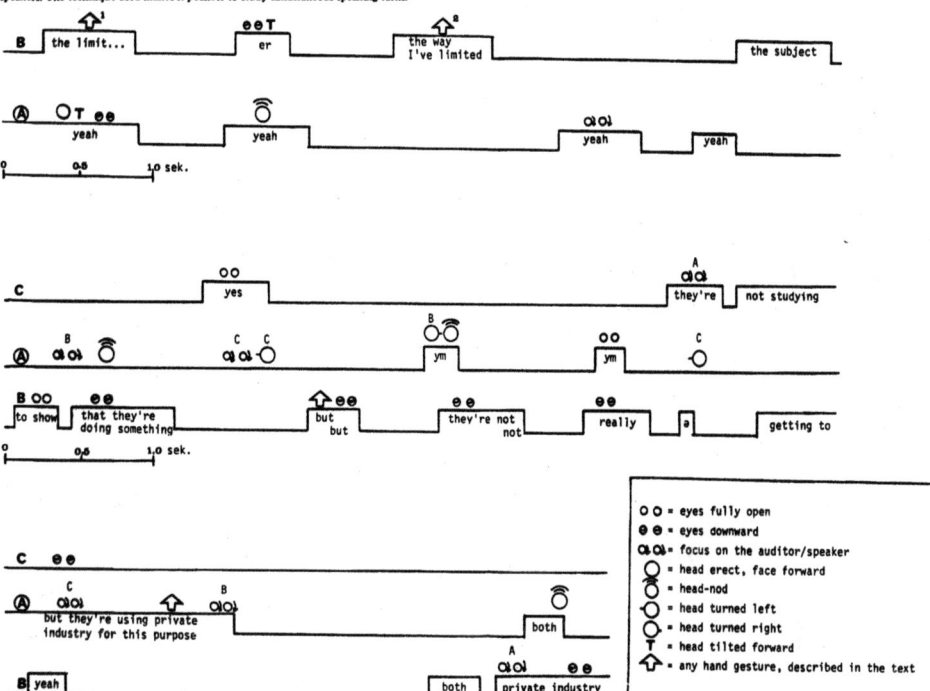

parameters which are derived from the videotape. The complete map resembles the three strips reproduced in Figure 1. In addition, the audiotape on which each participant's utterances are recorded separately can be used for the instrumental analysis of various paralinguistic features such as stress and intonation (for a more detailed discussion see Sajavaara, Lehtonen and Korpimies, 1979); see also Sajavaara, 1978a).

The Concept of Fluency: Tests with Some Tentative Parameters

Among the goals of foreign language teaching, 'fluency of speech' is one of the most popular. It is used to define the objective at the level of oral communication. As a concept 'fluency' is, however, vague and the definitions which are available are often contradictory. Even in contexts where disfluencies of patients with speech defects are discussed, the meaning of the point of reference, i.e. fluent speech, has not normally been defined. At the receptive end of language skills, the ability to understand messages spoken 'at a normal rate of delivery' is the counterpart of fluency in speech production; both of them lack any objective definition.

Fluency is one of the criteria which are given as parameters of a good native or native-like language-behaviour. The word is used in a variety of meanings and it is obvious that a loose application of the term to what might be termed as 'constant flow of speech' or 'periods of relative speech continuity' (see, e.g., Henderson, 1974 : 122) has been among the most prominent. Temporal and sequential aspects of speech production are emphasized in most cases. Connected with the fact that judgements as to what is fluent and what is not fluent — even what is a pause — tend to be highly subjective, the ambiguity of the term 'fluency' may often result in a dubious assessment of the FL behaviour of language students. As a matter of fact, there are several grammatical, pragmatic, and extralinguistic factors which are involved in our impression of 'fluency' of speech (for a detailed discussion of the problems of fluency and foreign language teaching, see Leeson, 1975, and Sajavaara and Lehtonen, 1979). For several reasons it seems appropriate to try to define fluency as correlated to the normal tempo of speech:

(1) In foreign language teaching it is necessary to specify the aims of the teaching more concretely. It is vital to know what is 'fluent speech' and what are the distinguishing marks of non-fluent speech.

(2) Teaching material that is meant for listening purposes has to meet the criterion of fluency and the criterion of normal speech rate. But it is a difficult task for a non-native teacher to judge whether a speech sample of a foreign language meant for listening is spoken fluently and at a normal speech rate.

(3) It is important to know the reference of the concepts 'fluent speech' and 'normal speech rate' when planning or standardizing the methods of language testing.

(4) It would be of great value if a measurable parameter could be found to be used to define the fluency of each pupil's speech. It would be of still greater value if fluency could be automatically measured on the basis of certain phenomena of physical speech.

Reading tests are a popular method of analyzing verbal fluency and its disorders in speakers of various sub-groups of the speech community (children, psychiatric patients, people with speech defects, patients with various diseases, etc.). It seems therefore appropriate to discuss the applicability of reading tests to the evaluation of oral fluency in a foreign language by comparing the results obtained from reading tests and tests of free delivery of speech with speakers of two languages and with speakers at different stages of foreign language studies.

Speech rate and pauses have recently been examined from various points of view. They are central variables in the testing of speech processing and constraints upon it both in the production and perception of speech. Phonetic evidence for different syntactic theories and hypotheses has been sought in pauses; pauses and tempo of speech are traditional variables in studies where the discourse between a psychiatrist and his patient is analyzed, as well as in those contrasting normal and pathological speech, and in studies where the evaluation parameters of fluent and non-fluent speech are defined. Speech rate and pauses are central variables from the point of view of foreign language teaching as well. Too fast a speech rate, and, above all, the lack of pauses or the occurrence of syntactically inappropriate pauses can be fatal to the understanding of the student's foreign language. It also appears that the interference from the student's mother tongue even affects pausing and the rate of speech and that the level of the student's oral skills in a foreign language can to some extent be expressed by figures indicating the rate of speech and the percentage of pauses (cf. Lehtonen, 1979; Raupach, forthcoming).

The Jyväskylä Finnish-English Contrastive Project (see Sajavaara and Lehtonen, 1978a) has carried out a number of tests to correlate the communicative behaviour of Finnish speakers of English with that of native speakers. Since material in which Finns' performance is contrasted with that of native speakers may lead to faulty conclusions about the mother tongue's influence, it was considered necessary to expand the tests to comprise non-native speakers of English other than Finns. Several tests were carried out with speakers at different levels of language proficiency: university students of English; university students of other subjects who had studied English at school before they were admitted to the university; students at various commercial colleges whose native language was Finnish, Finland Swedish, or Swedish; and British and American native speakers of English.

Parameters relating to the structure of the text analysed, such as false starts, spoonerisms, imprecisions, filled pauses, lexical density, type/token ratio, sentence and clause length, and subordination index, which are among the classical parameters used to describe fluency of utterances, will not be taken into account below (cf., however, Sajavaara and Lehtonen, 1978b). Neither has pausing been analysed functionally by classifying the physical (unfilled) pauses into permissible or acceptable juncture pauses and into hesitation pauses which cause disfluency. Accordingly, the occurrence of filled pauses and pause fillers (such as the vocalization *er* or extraneous words *well, now, you see, I mean*, etc.) in speech of the different groups of informants have not been analyzed systematically. Phonetic transfer of the mother tongue to the English of the informants is not touched upon at all. In each test group, interference caused by the mother tongue is indisputable, and the 'foreign accent' is characteristically different in the test groups.[1]

Two kinds of tests were carried out: reading tests and tests of free or spontaneous delivery of speech. The speaking tests consisted of short oral descriptions of textless cartoons. The informants were given a short summary of the content of the cartoon to read before they were asked to narrate the content. The summaries served to make the narrations more homogenous in their content and length.

Two of the phonetic parameters of fluency were analyzed: the rate of speech and the pause ratio. The following discussion concerns these two only.[2] The pauses and the rate were measured by means of an automatic counter which did not distinguish between juncture pauses and hesitation pauses. Both in the speech of the Finnish students and in the speech of the native speakers the percentage of pauses out of the total duration was much higher in spontaneous speech than in reading. In reading the percentage of pauses did not distinguish the two groups of Finnish speakers of English, while in free speech the three groups of speakers differed markedly as concerns the amount of pause time: the Finnish business college students have pauses up to 56 %, university students to 51 %, and the native speakers to 37 % of the total time (see Figure 2). The higher amount of pause time for the students was not a transfer from the mother tongue, because in free speech in their native language the percentages are close

---

1   For typical 'errors' made by Finns in the pronunciation of English, see Suomi, 1976; Lehtonen, Sajavaara and May, 1977; Lehtonen and Sajavaara (eds.), 1979.

2   On the basis of what fluency is generally expected to be (i.e. various temporal and sequential phenomena of speech performance), native speaker performance should be characterized by relative speech continuity, non-appearance of failures to complete sentences, varied vocabulary, rather elaborate sentence structures, precise expressions, and scarcity of extraneous words and phrases. In the preliminary tests it turned out that these features were more prominent in Finnish English speech than in native English speech. There were two notable exceptions: the number of pauses and the subordination index (see Sajavaara and Lehtonen, 1978b).

to those of the British speakers. Thus, the percentage of pauses seems to be one of the options for a phonetic parameter of fluency in free speech but not in reading. The individual variation in acceptable pausing is, however, high in free speech, and the instrumental method applied is unable to classifiy the pauses into hesitation and acceptable grammatical, juncture, or rhythmic pauses. Pausing was found to be one of the problems of a Finnish speaker of English. The total rate of speech of Finnish-speaking Finns is dramatically lower and the percentage of pauses higher than those of Swedish-speaking Finns and Swedes. Even the advanced Finnish students of English were behind the Swedish group with less training in English.

Although the material has not yet been analyzed as regards the placing of pauses, preliminary findings seem to indicate that the Finnish-speaking Finns differ from the other groups quite distinctly in this respect. In the English spoken by Finns the placement of pauses is sporadic in relation to the syntactic structure of the sentences. The Finnish informants often place the pauses in such a way that it breaks the constituent structure of the sentence. This is not found in the English of the Swedish-speaking informants. As stated in a paper dealing with the signalling of word boundaries (Lehtonen and Koponen, 1977), inconsistency in the English of Finns in the placement of pauses and in the signalling of word boundaries may indirectly reflect the way in which a Finn processes the phonetic flow of speech into semantic units in perception. The 'errors' made in pausing and in the phonetic grouping of the message for production may correspond to a confusion in perceptual processes when listening to spoken English. A more detailed analysis of the material will certainly give further information in this respect.

The correlation between speech rhythm and fluent speech was also studied in connection with the tests mentioned above, because it has sometimes been suggested that rhythm is a primary factor in fluent speech. The experiments showed clearly (see Lehtonen, 1978b) that fluency and rhythm have little correlation with the physical variation of sequences of voice and pauses in speech. Since, in addition to a temporal sequencing of speech flow, repetition of intonation patterns with a certain regularity might be involved in the effect of speech rhythm, this aspect was also taken into consideration. The results however were negative, and the final conclusion was that neither the alternation of speech sequences and pauses nor the intonation patterns as such offer a solution to the problem of fluency. The results of the measurements of speech rate can be summarized as follows: in all groups, the rate of reading was clearly higher than the rate of speaking, both in the informants' mother tongue and in English. This was true both as regards the total rate, where the difference, due to longer and more frequent pauses in free speech, was dramatic, and as regards the articulation rate. However, when the Finns, the Swedish-speaking Finns, and the Swedes spoke English, the difference in the articulation rate between free delivery and reading was greater than that of the British and American speakers (the ratio of Finns 1 : 1.24, Swedish-speaking Finns 1 : 1.24, Swedes 1 : 1.12, but Britons 1 : 1.05, and Americans 1 : 1.02). Since the distribution in the articulation rate

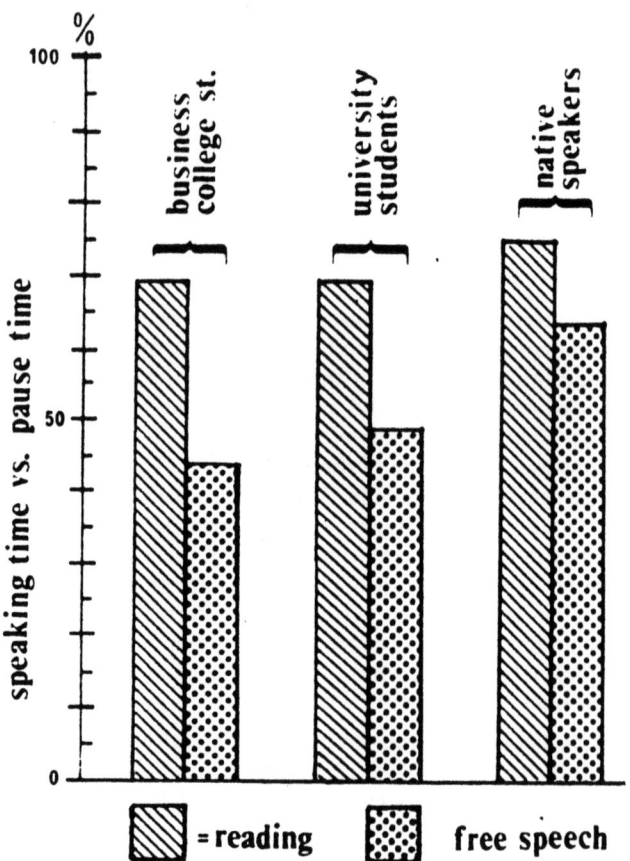

FIGURE 2

The distribution of the actual speech performance (articulation) and pauses in the total speaking time in the English speech of three groups of speakers. The pause time was calculated automatically by means of an electronic device which counts as a pause each voiceless sequence of speech which is longer than a given threshold (0.2 seconds). The pairs of bars show the articulation time/pause time ratios as a percentage of articulation time out of the total time of *reading* (striped columns) and *spontaneous speech* (dotted columns). The first pair of columns on the left shows the pause ratio in English spoken by Finnish students of a commercial college (N=24), those in the middle that of Finnish university students of English, on the right the ratio of six native speakers of English. (Lehtonen, 1978a.)

of free delivery in particular was great among the native speakers, some of them actually produced speech faster when speaking spontaneously than when reading. The rate of articulation was clearly slower in the English of all the student groups than in the native speakers' English.

In articulation rate the advanced Finnish students almost reached the level of native speakers. In the total rate of reading the standard passage they do not attain the 'satisfactory' level on the Fairbanks rating scale (the British speakers obtain the rating 'excellent'), and the figures of the commercial college students remain far below the bottom of the scale. It is noteworthy that there is considerable variation in the articulation rates of advanced students: some of them have reached the typical speed of a native speaker and even 'shoot over'. This type of overshoot also appears elsewhere in the pronunciation of advanced students. The student when striving for native-like fluency links words together, reduces and swallows unstressed syllables more than the native speaker does. In the cross-language comparison, Swedish-speaking Finns and the Swedes obtained the rating 'too slow', and the Finnish Business College students remained far below the bottom of the scale. The Finnish-speaking university students of English obtained a result (c. 140 wpm) which would also be rated 'too slow' on the Fairbanks scale.

It is obvious that fluency is a vague concept. At least two aspects are combined in it: linguistic acceptability and smooth continuity of speech. Fluency seems to equal the communicative acceptability of the speech act ('communicative fit'): its qualities or the demands set upon it cannot be defined from the point of view of the actual message (i.e. the text) since the expectations concerning it vary according to the communicative situation. Thus there is no 'normal' speech rate, nor a 'correct' number of pauses typical of fluent speech. The normal speech rate cannot be considered to be an absolute value that could be defined as a number of words or syllables per time unit; the expectations concerning the normal speech rate, for example, of a sports commentary or a Christmas sermon are quite different. Another variable which affects the expectations for the normal speech rate is the level of abstraction and referential complexity of the text. The expectations also depend on the communicative situation. Therefore, the methods of measuring the phonetic parameters of fluency can be applied to evaluating or rating foreign language students' speech only if all of these variables are closely controlled. And even then, the figures discussed above can only be applied in a very broad testing of the command of spoken language.

Learning to speak fluently means above all learning that, in different situations, different communicative registers are used. Fluency does not always imply an uninterrupted flow of speech which is sequentially and grammatically irreproachable. To be fluent in the right way, the speaker has to know how to hesitate, how to be silent, how to self-correct, how to interrupt, and how to complete his expressions. According to this definition of fluency, speech must meet the expectations of the speech community and represent normal, acceptable and relaxed language behaviour. Testing of such a quality of speech is not possible by means of any instrumental method.

Conclusion

In studying language behaviour, we must remember that communication is a two-way phenomenon, and a speaker's performance is conditioned by what the hearer does or does not do, i.e. by the linguistic and other cues which the hearer receives from the speaker and produces in connection with the communicative act. In a communicative situation, a person normally assumes several roles: social, textual and participatory roles. For FL speakers the social roles are rather restricted: in most cases the typical situation is a stranger talking to a stranger and most of the social criteria found in connection with L1 do not apply. The greater number of the social roles are reduced to a foreigner's role, which also means that native speaker's expectations are quite different from what they are towards other native speakers. A foreigner may, for instance, be given more time for the formulation of his message. The conversational mechanisms which govern the interchange of textual roles, i.e. the turntaking system, do not, obviously, function in the same way as they function between native speakers: a native speaker talking to a non-native speaker is more prepared to wind up the non-native speaker's sentences during and after hesitations and pauses and to give reformulations.

A non-native speaker seldom achieves a symmetrical position with regard to the native speaker (see Ventola, 1977); this is, moreover, not uncommon between native speakers. A non-native speaker talking to a native speaker retains, in most cases, the participatory role of the respondent; he is less active, and more willing to cede the role of the initiator to the native speaker. It is to be expected that a non-native speaker's role as a foreigner and a respondent will influence reactions to what we have described as parameters of fluency.

If contrastive analysis is defined as meaning the comparison of the structures of two languages (i.e. two communicative systems), it is necessary to adopt a concept of communicative structures, and such structures involve phenomena that go beyond mere grammatical structures. The objective of contrastive analysis should simultaneously be expanded to the establishment of the similarities and differences in the way in which ideas and messages are conveyed through the chains of communication in the two or more languages (see also Sajavaara, 1977).

Traditional linguistic contrastive research is still necessary for gathering information about various subdisciplines of linguistic analysis (phonetics, syntax, semantics, lexicon, and text), but the intelligibility of messages must be studied in communicative situations with respect to various criteria drawn from these subdisciplines. Research in which both correct and deviant elements are observed is needed on the L1 and L2 discourse of the same informants.

Psycholinguistic and sociolinguistic research is needed on the decisions which a speaker-hearer is expected to make to produce acceptable utterances in given social situations. The influence of insufficient competence on communication should be studied, including the total effect of fluency and disfluency. Contrastive information is needed on the influence of the variation of the two languages on the cross-language phenomena, as well as on the roles of the speaker-hearer and the norms affecting the speech situation. Various attitudinal and emotive factors also need to be investigated.

By methods which have been discussed above, it may be possible to specify the features which characterize native and non-native speaker performance, important for cross-language communication. It would be a crude simplification of the real state of affairs to believe that good language competence is always materialized in fluent speech. A person who may govern the nuances and complexities of literary expression skillfully may be incapable of good speech performance, and another person whose vocabulary and command of structural options are rather restricted may be able to carry out fairly efficient communication by using the restricted means of expression with great skill. If a communicative fit means that the communicative processes meet the listener's expectation, what is needed for the assessment of fluency is an appraisal of what sort of responses various phenomena in a speaker's performance trigger in the hearer. It is not necessary to pay much attention to the correctness of grammatical structures and absence of grammatical errors. Teaching proper language behaviour involves teaching the pragmatics of a given language. In this respect there is not much difference in the mother tongue and in foreign languages. A speaker who commands the communicative strategies in the proper way is able to overcome the critical moments in the flow of communication, while 'strategy failures' in the processing of communication result in disruptions.

REFERENCES

CLARK, H.H. and E.V. Clark 1977. *Psychology and Language: An Introduction to Psycholinguistics.* New York: Harcourt, Brace, Jovanovich.

DAVIS, S.M. 1978. Audition and Speech Perception. In: R.L. Schiefelbusch (ed.). *Bases of Language Intervention.* Baltimore: University Park Press.

FILLMORE, L.W. 1976. *The Second Time Around: Cognitive and Social Strategies in Second Language Acquisition.* Ph.D. Dissertation. Stanford.

FISIAK, J. 1973. The Polish-English Contrastive Project. In: J. Fisiak (ed.). *Papers and Studies in Contrastive Linguistics* 1. Poznań: Adam Mickiewicz University, 5-13.

FISIAK, J., M. Grzegorek-Lipinska and T. Zabrocki 1978. *An Introductory English-Polish Contrastive Grammar.* Warszawa: PWN.

FRITH, M.B. 1976. *Second Language Learning: A Study of Form and Function at Two Stages of Developing Interlanguage.* Bloomington, Ind.: Indiana University Linguistics Club.

HAKUTA, K. and H. Cancino 1977. Trends in Second Language Acquisition Research. *Harvard Educational Review.* 47, 294-316.

HATCH, E. 1977. Second Language Learning. In: *Bilingual Education: Current Perspectives/Linguistics.* Arlington, Va.: Center for Applied Linguistics, 60-86.

HENDERSON, A.I. 1974. Time Patterns in Spontaneous Speech – Cognitive Stride or Random Walk? A Reply to Jaffe et al. (1972). *Language and Speech.* 17, 119-125.

KRASHEN, S.D. 1977. Some Issues Relating to the Monitor Model. In: H.D. Brown, C.A. Yorio and R.H. Crymes (eds.). *On TESOL '77: Teaching and Learning English as a Second Language: Trends in Research and Practice.* Washington, D.C.: TESOL, 144-158.

KRASHEN, S.D. 1978. Adult Second Language Acquisition and Learning: A Review of Theory and Applications. Paper read at the Second Language Acquisition and Foreign Language Teaching Conference, Silver Spring, Maryland. March 10-11, 1978.

KRZESZOWSKI, T.P. 1974. *A Contrastive Generative Grammar.* Lódz: University of Lódz.

LABOV, W. 1970. *The Study of Non-standard English.* Urbana. I11.: National Council of Teachers of English.

LADEFOGED, P. 1977. Communicative and Linguistic Aspects of Speech Production. In: M. Sawashina and F.S. Cooper (eds.). *Dynamic Aspects of Speech Production*. University of Tokyo Press, 409-410.

LAMENDELLA, J. 1977. The Limbic System in Human Communication. In: H. Whitaker and H.A. Whitaker (eds.) *Studies in Neurolinguistics*. Vol. 3. New York: Academic Press, 157-222.

LEESON, R. 1975. *Fluency and Language Teaching*. London: Longman.

LEHTONEN, J. 1978a. Problems of Measuring Fluency and Normal Rate of Speech. Paper read at the 5th International Congress of Applied Linguistics. Montreal, August, 1978. Forthcoming.

LEHTONEN, J. 1978b. On the Problems of Measuring Fluency. In: M. Leiwo and A. Räsänen (eds.). *AFinLA:n vuosikirja 1978*, Publications de l'Association Finlandaise de Linguistique Appliquée 23, 53-68.

LEHTONEN, J. 1978c. How Can the Theory and Methods of Speech Sciences Contribute to Contrastive Analysis. Paper read at the 16th International Conference on Polish-English Contrastive Linguistics. Boszkowo, Poland, December, 1978.

LEHTONEN, J. 1979. Speech Rate and Pauses in the English of Finns, Swedish-speaking Finns, and Swedes. In: H. Ringbom and R. Palmberg (eds.). *Papers on Error Analysis*, Engelska Institutionens vid Åbo Akademi publikationer 6. Åbo 1979.

LEHTONEN, J. and M. Koponen 1977. Signalling of Morphophonological Boundaries by Finnish Speakers of English: Preliminary Findings. In: K. Sajavaara and J. Lehtonen (eds.). *Contrastive Papers*, Jyväskylä Contrastive Studies 4. Jyväskylä: Department of English, University of Jyväskylä, 75-87.

LEHTONEN, J. and K. Sajavaara (eds.) 1979. *Papers in Contrastive Phonetics*. Jyväskylä Contrastive Studies 7. Jyväskylä: Department of English, University of Jyväskylä.

LEHTONEN, J., K. Sajavaara and A. May 1977. *Spoken English: The Perception and Production of English on a Finnish-English Contrastive Basis*. Jyväskylä: Gummerus.

MAHL, G. 1972. People Talking When They Can't Hear their Voices. In: A. Siegman and B. Pope (eds.). *Studies in Dyadic Communication*. New York: Pergamon Press.

MARSLEN-WILSON, W.D. and A. Welsh 1978. Processing Interaction and Lexical Access during Word Recognition in Continuous Speech. *Cognitive Psychology*. 10, 29-63.

RAUPACH, M. forthcoming. Temporal Variables in First and Second Language Speech Production. In: H.W. Dechert and M. Raupach (eds.). *Temporal Variables in Speech*. The Hague: Mouton.

SAJAVAARA, K. 1977. Contrastive Linguistics Past and Present and a Communicative Approach. In: K. Sajavaara and J. Lehtonen (eds.). *Contrastive Papers* 4, Jyväskylä: Department of English, University of Jyväskylä, 9-30.

SAJAVAARA, K. 1978a. Expanding the Contrastive Analysis Framework. Paper read at the Third International Colloquium of Contrastive Linguistics and Translation Science. Trier and Saarbrücken, September 1978.

SAJAVAARA, K. 1978b. The Monitor Model and Contrastive Analysis. Paper read at the 16th International Conference of Polish-English Contrastive Linguistics, Boszkowo, Poland, December, 1978. Forthcoming.

SAJAVAARA, K. and J. Lehtonen 1978a. The Finnish-English Contrastive Project: Status and Progress Report. In: K. Sajavaara and J. Lehtonen (eds.). *Further Contrastive Papers*, Jyväskylä Contrastive Studies 6, Jyväskylä: Department of English, University of Jyväskylä: 7-30.

SAJAVAARA, K. and J. Lehtonen 1978b. Spoken Language and the Concept of Fluency. In: L. Lautamatti and P. Lindquist (eds.). *Focus on Spoken Language*, Special Issue of *Language Centre News*, Jyväskylä: Language Centre for Finnish Universities, 23-57.

SAJAVAARA, K. and J. Lehtonen 1979. *Fluency and Communicative Competence*. Forthcoming.

SAJAVAARA, K., J. Lehtonen and L. Korpimies 1979. The Methodology and Practice of Contrastive Discourse Analysis. In: K. Sajavaara and J. Lehtonen (eds.). *Papers in Contrastive Discourse Analysis*, Jyväskylä Contrastive Studies 5, Jyväskylä: Department of English, University of Jyväskylä.

SNOW, C. and C. Ferguson (eds.) 1977. *Talking to Children*. New York: Cambridge University Press.

SUOMI, K. 1976. *English Voiceless and Voiced Stops as Produced by Finnish and Native Speakers*. Jyväskylä Contrastive Studies 2. Jyväskylä: Department of English, University of Jyväskylä.

VENTOLA, E. 1977. *On the Structure and Management of Casual Conversations*. M.A. Thesis. Sydney: Macquarie University.

VENTOLA, E. 1978. *A Study of Conversational Strategies in Finnish and English*, M.A. Thesis. Jyväskylä: University of Jyväskylä.

WATERSON, N. and C. Snow (eds.) 1978. *The Development of Communication*. New York: Wiley.

WODE, H. 1978. L2 Research Activities in Germany. *SLANT* 8, 1 (May), 22-28.

REPETITION AND CORRECTION AS AN INDICATION OF SPEECH PLANNING AND EXECUTION PROCESSES AMONG SECOND LANGUAGE LEARNERS

Ann K. Fathman
Rochester, Minnesota

The study of errors produced in speech has frequently been used in the field of psycholinguistics as a means of studying language planning and execution processes. The analysis of errors and their correction have, for example, been used to examine developmental changes in children's first language (Rogers, 1978), children's awareness of language (Clark, 1977), the relationship between performance and competence (Fromkin, 1973). Other first language speech behaviors, such as hesitation pauses (Goldman-Eisler, 1968; Boomer, 1965; Butterworth, 1975) and repeats (Maclay and Osgood, 1959) have been used to examine semantic planning, grammatical encoding and other production processes. These studies demonstrate that perhaps "more information is to be got out of the act of speaking than the verbal content of the linguistic product." (Goldman-Eisler, 1968)

In second language research, the focus has in the past been on the product rather than the process of speech production (see Tarone, Swain, Fathman, 1976, for further discussion). Seliger (1978) has recently suggested, however, that the analysis of certain speech production behaviors, which have been overlooked in second language research until now, may provide valuable data about language learning. He suggests that behaviors such as hesitations, repeats, the use of intonation contours and self-corrections in spontaneous speech could tell us more about the underlying processes of hypothesis testing and utterance planning. His preliminary analysis of the use of question intonations and pauses by adult second language learners illustrates how covert planning may be inferred from overt performance. Dechert (forthcoming) has suggested that a cross-linguistic approach to the study of such behaviors in spontaneous speech may provide a clearer picture of the processes involved in learning a second language.

In this study, two of these behaviors, repetitions and self-initiated corrections, are examined in the speech of second language learners. The kinds of corrections and location of repetitions and corrections within the utterance are analyzed to illustrate where planning takes place, what hypotheses are being confirmed or rejected, and the extent to which native language interferes with utterance planning in lexicon retrieval and syntactic organization. Three general questions are asked:

1) What kinds of self-initiated repetitions and corrections are made by second language learners?
2) What kinds of underlying processes of production might be inferred from these repetitions and corrections?
3) How does one's first language (L1) interfere with utterance planning and execution in the production of a second language (L2)?

Method

To obtain the speech samples for this study, approximately 75 children between the ages of 8 and 11 were interviewed. The children were studying in public schools in the U.S., but English was their second language. Twenty-five of the children were native Korean speakers and fifty were native Spanish speakers. All of the children spoke their native language at home, but were quite proficient at English. All subjects had been in the U.S. and American schools at least one year.

Each child was spoken with individually for about 15 minutes; the interview was recorded on tape and later transcribed. All children were asked a number of personal information questions and then asked to tell a story about a number of pictures.

Interviews in both English and Spanish were given to the native Spanish speakers to provide L1 and L2 speech samples for the same individuals. All of the interviews were kept as similar and informal as possible. The children were never prompted or corrected by the interviewer.

The self-initiated repetitions and corrections made by these children in L1 and L2 provide the data discussed in this paper. Both repetitions and corrections are examined since it is felt that both can serve as indicators of the language planning process. 'Repetition' refers to the repeating of the same utterance (or its parts) more than once; while 'correction' refers to the repeating of an utterance (or its parts), with changes made in structure or meaning.

The Repetitions

The repeats made by the children during the interviews were categorized into two groups: 1) the repetition of correct forms, 2) the repetition of incorrect forms. Approximately 98 % of all repeated utterances (or parts of utterances) were correct. An incorrect utterance was almost never repeated without changes being made.

Most of the repeats involved the repetition of one or two words, followed by the completion of an utterance. Entire utterances were almost never repeated. Examples of common repetitions are given in Table 1.

Table 1: Examples of Repetitions

Original utterance	Repeat
then he...	then he started to cry
the...	the little boy sit
I...	I'm go to grandma
I have...	I have 4 sisters
and the boy...	the boy got...got hot...hot

About 90 % of the 75 repetitions analyzed occurred after the first or second word of a constituent beginning an utterance. There was almost always a pause made between the original utterance and repeat. Maclay and Osgood (1959) in studying silent pauses and repeats and Boomer (1965) in his study of pauses made by L1 speakers have noted similar locations for pauses and repeats in their data.

If pauses and repeats are indicative of certain aspects of speech planning, then there appear to be similarities in planning whether one is speaking a first or second language. The repetitions described in Table 1 probably allow the speaker time to plan for the next part of the utterance and occur at points where dicisions are being made about what should follow in the utterance. The fact that they most often occur after the first or second function word and before a content word suggests that semantic (topic selection or general meaning) and syntactic planning may take place before the precise lexical items have been selected (see Seliger 1978 for a more detailed discussion). The location of these repetitions would suggest then that second language learners frequently begin to speak without having planned *in detail* the make-up of the constituents.

Repeats most likely also serve other functions in the speech of L2 learners. The repetition of an utterance or its parts may be an indication of monitoring (in terms of correctness) by the L2 speaker of his speech. A learner may produce an utterance, reconsider what he has said and repeat it when he is satisfied that it is correct or serves the communication function that he desires. This may be the reason for the infrequent repetition of whole constituents such as: 1) and then the cat went...then the cat went somewhere, 2) if I do my homework...I do my homework. In examples as 1 and 2, hesitation and repetition occur after content words have been selected.

An utterance may also be repeated to emphasize what is being said or to draw the attention of the person being addressed to a particular point. A more thorough analysis of the contexts and make-up of repetition is necessary before exact functions can be determined.

The Corrections

The self-initiated corrections analyzed in this study include the correction of errors which are the result of the production of incorrect forms and the correction of errors which are linguistically permissable but semantically inappropriate for communicating the ideas of the speaker. The corrections made in the speech of these second language learners were frequently false starts where one or more words were corrected. Both retraced false starts (where 1 or more words were repeated before the correction as in 1) and unretraced false starts (no words were repeated before the correction as in 2).

1) the mother is seeing the baby —▷ is seeing what they're doing
2) I saw a big dog —▷ cat

Unlike repetitions, the corrections did not occur regularly at any one part of an utterance or constituent, as examples 3 through 6 illustrate:

3) he is here —▷ she is here
4) he have —▷ he has a cat
5) there's a cat off a tree —▷ on a tree
6) he has 2 book —▷ he has 2 books

If self-corrections are an indication of hypothesis testing, the different locations of the corrections would suggest that second language learners monitor their speech productions as much at the end and middle of an utterance as at the beginning. While speaking, the L2 speaker is editing what he is saying and how he is saying it. If at any point during an utterance he is aware of a mistake in his speech, he will stop and attempt to correct or clarify what he has said to better communicate his ideas. However, most L2 speakers probably do not correct themselves every time that they are aware an error has been made, for in spontaneous speech, the press for fluent expression forces a speaker to keep up the pace of his speech to make himself understood and to hold the attention of the person he is adressing.

Some corrections were preceded by unfilled pauses, but these pauses were in general shorter than pauses occurring between repeats, indicating perhaps that corrections do not serve the same planning function as hesitations and repeats.

The corrections appearing in these speech samples have been divided into 5 types and in Table 2 examples of each type are given. Type I corrections are corrections of phonology. Tape II corrections are corrections of morphology without a change in emphasis or meaning. Type III corrections are corrections of syntax where word order is changed without a change in meaning. Type IV corrections are changes in the meaning of the utterance in general or topic changes. These corrections are usually preceded by words such as: 'I mean', 'no'. Type V corrections are corrections of lexicon where one or two words are changes in an utterance.

Table 2

Examples of Self-corrections

Type I phonological changes	I was looking to a 'kit' —▷ in the 'riving' room —▷	a 'cat' in the 'living' room
Type II morphological changes	I live here 2 year —▷ the cat is sit —▷	2 years is sitting in the chair
Type III syntactic changes	The boy's going to make off the cat —▷ take the cat off the tree He give to apple the boy —▷ He give to boy the apple	
Type IV changes in meaning of utterance	Daddy went home —▷ Two girls playing ball —▷	I mean, went to work and came home No, girl giving her sister a ball
Type V changes in words used	people who couldn't talk —▷ the boy —▷	who couldn't understand the children are coming

Corrections of each type were made by these L2 learners, but some types occurred more frequently than others. It was found that corrections involved either the omission, addition, replacement or re-ordering of elements within an utterance. The number of corrections of each type which occurred in the data are given in Table 3.

Table 3

Number of self-corrections of different types produced by L2 speakers

Type of correction	omission	addition	substitution/ replacement	re-ordering
I – phonological		1	3	
II – morphological	1	8	14	
III – syntactic			8	6
IV – semantic		3	15	
V – lexical	2	10	45	

The greatest number of corrections were changes in lexical items. As is shown in Table 3, about 40 % of all corrections were substitutions of one word for another – usually one content word for another. The large number of corrections of lexicon suggests that before an utterance is made, planning may not be complete in terms of the exact lexical items which will be used. Thus frequently, the word first spontaneously uttered does not satisfy the features that the speaker wants to express so another word is substituted. The speaker may also be more aware of incorrect lexical items than morphological or syntactic errors which in this analysis are not associated with changes in meaning. Thus, changes in lexicon are made due to the high information content and ease with which word substitutions can be made.

The corrections which involved the change in topic or meaning of the entire utterance (Type IV corrections) seem to be the result of two phenomena: either the speaker realizes he has given incorrect information and proceeds to correct himself, or he realizes that he cannot adequately express the information he wishes to in L2 and changes the topic or focus of what he is saying.

The fact that the most frequent kind of corrections on all levels were substitutions suggests that the general ordering and number of constituents in an utterance is outlined in the mind of the speaker before speaking. Additions, omissions or re-ordering seldom occur during the speech act, but primarily substitutions are made in slots which have been pre-planned.

Influence of L1 on L2 Speech Behaviors

The influence of L1 on L2 production is examined by comparing: 1) the kinds and number of repetitions and corrections made by L2 learners from different language backgrounds (Korean and Spanish), and 2) the repetitions and corrections made by the same individuals in their first language, Spanish, and their second language, English.

The greatest number of corrections were 'word substitutions' for both the Korean and Spanish children. The interference of Lexicon into L2 speech was apparent in only two cases (both Spanish):

1) there is the father and niño —▷ boy
2) I have duo —▷ two sisters

There were other kinds of errors made which were obviously related to L1 but which were not corrected by the children (for example, frequent omission of the article by the Korean children). The Korean children did make almost four times as many corrections of bound morpheme errors, as in 3:

3) The girl is clean —▷ is cleaning

This may be related to the fact that they were more concerned with producing grammatically correct forms or that they initially made more errors in bound morphemes and this resulted in more corrections of this type. A more detailed analysis of the kinds and numbers of errors produced may provide further information about the reasons why certain self-corrections are made.

There were no other differences noted in the kinds of self-corrections made by the two language groups, suggesting that language background does not greatly influence the kinds of corrections made.

The total number of repetitions and corrections made by Korean and Spanish children did vary, however, as shown in Table 4.

Table 4

Average number of repetitions and corrections made per student

	Repetition	Correction
Spanish	.5	1.4
Korean	2.3	2.2

The Koreans made more repetitions and corrections in their speech. They, in general, seemed less confident in speaking English and more concerned about errors they were making. They took longer to respond and hesitated more, indicating more speech planning than the Spanish, who spoke quite spontaneously. Thus, culturally related learner characteristics probably have an effect on speech planning processes and should not be overlooked when comparisons are being made between different second language learners. These differences may be related to the differences noted in cognitive style by Seliger (1978a) among the adult second language learners he studied.

The speech of the native Spanish-speaking children in the Spanish and English interviews was compared to determine if the children tended to make similar kinds of corrections and repetitions in L1 as in L2. There were fewer corrections made in the L1 Spanish interviews since the children were speaking their native language and made fewer errors in general. However, the kinds of corrections did appear to be similar; most corrections in L1, as in L2, involved changes in lexicon as in 4. Many of the corrections in lexicon in the Spanish interviews involved changes from English to Spanish words as in 5 and 6.

4) la niña esta agarrando a la mama —▷ a la maestra
5) estaba en recess —▷ recreo
6) una señora esta carry —▷ cargando una niña

Surprisingly, there was a great deal more interference of English lexicon into the speech of these native Spanish speakers than interference of Spanish into their English. Frequently in speaking Spanish an English word was used, and it appeared that only after the word was produced did the speaker realize that he had spoken English and proceed to make a correction. This interference was primarily evidenced in the lexicon, and suggests that when a language is learned and used in a 'natural setting', as at this English speaking school, there is a competing between systems and lexical retrieval in the native language may be affected.

Summary

The results of this preliminary analysis of the speech of second language learners can be summarized in terms of the questions initially asked:

1) Most repetitions in L2 speech involve repeats of one or two words followed by the completion of an utterance. These repeats usually occur after the first or second function word of a constituent beginning an utterance. These repetitions probably allow the speaker time to plan for the next part of the utterance — usually a content word. The fact that they occur after a constituent has been begun suggests that perhaps general semantic and syntactic planning have already taken place and that it is the exact lexical items which are still being decided upon during speech execution.

2) Self-initiated corrections do not occur regularly at any one part of an utterance in L2 speech, indicating that the learner is continually monitoring what he is saying during a speech act. Most corrections involve the substitution of one word for another, suggesting that words spontaneously uttered do not satisfy the features the speaker wants to express; so another word is substituted. Subjects, in general, seemed more concerned about giving incorrect or inadequate information than with making structural errors in their speech for most corrections were semantic rather than structural in nature.

3) A comparison of the kinds of corrections made by the Korean and Spanish children, in their spoken English, showed that corrections of lexicon were most common for both language backgrounds. The Koreans did, however, make more morphological corrections than the Spanish speakers and repeated and corrected themselves more frequently. This suggests that there may be differences in cognitive style affecting speech production processes which are related to native language and cultural differences. The fact that L2 lexicon was frequently used in L1 speech by the Spanish suggests that in second language speech production, there is a competing between systems and, in terms of lexicon retrieval, the greatest effect may be on native language speech.

These results then suggest that there are regularities in the location and kinds of self-initiated repetitions and corrections made by second language learners when they speak. The analysis of such behaviors provides a means for examining the process of speech productions, and further study should provide valuable information about the speech planning and execution processes of second language learners from different linguistic and cultural backgrounds.

REFERENCES

BOOMER, D.S. 1965. Hesitation and Grammatical Encoding. *Language and Speech*. 8, 148-158.

BUTTERWORTH, B. 1975. Hesitation and Semantic Planning in Speech. *Journal of Psycholinguistic Research*. 4, 75-87.

CLARK, E.V. 1977. Awareness of Language: Some Evidence from What Children Say and Do. Paper presented at the Discussion Meeting on The Child's Conception of Language. Max-Planck-Gesellschaft. Nijmegen. The Netherlands.

CLARK, H.H. and E.V. Clark. 1977. *Psychology and Language: An Introduction to Psycholinguistics*. New York: Harcourt, Brace, Jovanovich.

DECHERT, H.W. forthcoming. Pauses and Intonation as Indicators of Verbal Planning in Second Language Speech Productions. In: H.W. Dechert and M. Raupach (eds.). *Temporal Variables in Speech*. The Hague: Mouton.

FROMKIN, V.A. (ed.). 1973. *Speech Errors as Linguistic Evidence*. The Hague: Mouton.

GOLDMAN-EISLER, F. 1968. *Psycholinguistics: Experiments in Spontaneous Speech*. New York: Academic Press.

MACLAY, H. and C.E. Osgood. 1959. Hesitation Phenomena in Spontaneous English Speech. *Word*. 15, 19-44.

ROGERS, S. 1978. Self-Initiated Corrections in the Speech of Infant-School Children. *Journal of Child Language*. 5, 365-371.

SELIGER, H. 1978. Hesitation and Speech Correction Behavior in L2 Learners. Paper presented at the Annual TESOL Convention. Mexico City, Mexico.

TARONE, E., M. Swain and A. Fathman. 1976. Some Limitations to the Classroom Applications of Current Second Language Acquisition Research. *TESOL Quarterly*. 10, 19-32.

UTTERANCE PLANNING AND CORRECTION BEHAVIOR: ITS FUNCTION IN THE GRAMMAR CONSTRUCTION PROCESS FOR SECOND LANGUAGE LEARNERS

Herbert W. Seliger
City University of New York

This study is concerned with the linguistic value of speech behavior. The term linguistic is used here to refer to the theory and grammar which internally is responsible for all of a speaker's output. Essentially, suggesting that such speech behavior is relevant for the study of linguistics is somewhat heretical in light of pronouncements by linguists of the generative-transformational view. Miller (1966), a psycholinguist, has cautioned against writing a grammar of mistakes.

Essentially these views derive from assuming an analogous relationship between physical capabilities and physical performance on the one hand and linguistic capabilities and linguistic performance on the other. The analogy is somewhat like the following: If we witnessed a man walking along the street who suddenly tripped and fell, we would obviously not assume that the man did not know how to walk or that the fall was any indication of any lack of that ability. What we witnessed was a momentary lapse in someone's ability to put into operation that which he knows. This man possessed the neuromuscular mechanisms to control walking and something external to his knowledge of walking was responsible for his tripping such as fatigue, an obstacle in his path or a muscle spasm.

By the same token, following the same analogy, language behavior or lapses in such behavior cannot be taken as any kind of indication of what underlies this behavior, namely competence. Lapses in utterances, self-corrections, slips of the tongue, repairs and hesitations of various kinds, while interesting to those involved in the study of utterance processing, are considered singularly uninteresting to the generative linguist. In his terms, such phenomena are "trivial". The term "trivial" is a technical term when used by the linguist to mean something which, while of some intrinsic interest, cannot contribute to the further development of linguistic theory. This opinion stems essentially from the view that such performance is not regular, rule governed and therefore not indicative of underlying knowledge in much the same way that tripping behavior is not indicative of the underlying knowledge one might have about walking.

It is not within the scope of this article to examine the validity of this point of view for second language acquisition. While it is the author's view that competence and performance may be more easily distinguished when one is dealing with the stable grammar of the native speaker or with a bilingual whose systems are no longer in state of flux, in the case of second language acquisition, it is difficult to capture the idea of an underlying competence distinct from performance simply because that competence grammar is in a constant state of flux. Competence based errors are not easily distinguished from lapses.

Therefore, the view proposed in this paper is that the study of a particular aspect of speech *performance* can be useful for understanding how competence *develops* and what its parameters may be at the time speech performance is sampled. To quote Goldman-Eisler (1968): "The study of spontaneous speech is essential if the aim of the enquiry is to gain an understanding of the generative process involved in speech production."

This study will be concerned with an analysis of the hesitation and speech correction behavior of second language (L2) learners and with the relevancy of such speech phenomena for understanding the language acquisition process. Speech correction and hesitation has been widely studied and, as witnessed by the current collection in this volume, is becoming widely recognized as an important source of psycholinguistic information. Many in the literature of psycholinguistics have looked at this side of language performance (for example, Maclay and Osgood, 1959; Goldman-Eisler, 1968; Garrett, 1975). However, no one to the knowledge of this writer has looked at the significance of this data for understanding the sentence planning strategies of adult second language learners.

The motivation for studying utterance planning and correction behavior (UPC) cross-linguistically may be described as follows:

1. Since such behavior is widely assumed to represent an attempt by the speaker, whether the speaker is a native speaker of the language or an L2 learner, to arrive at the ideal utterance, such study can reveal how the ideal is represented in the mind of the L2 learner. As with all human endeavors, there is often a problem between the planning stage and the execution stage. This is what leads all speakers to false starts, hesitations, and corrections. The difference between native speakers and L2 learners is of course with regard to *what* is corrected or repaired and *how*. It will be assumed here that correction reveals an awareness for the grammar of the language and the manner of planning and repair reveals the underlying processes or strategies utilized by the learner in the grammar construction process.

2. The attempts by the learner to reach the ideal form will also reveal what that ideal form may be. That is, UPC reveals the limits or extents of the L2 learners interlanguage. Such behavior will also reveal aspects of the storage systems of such speakers. As examples below will illustrate, UPC shows not only what grammar rules are functioning but how semantic information is stored in the grammar of the learner.

3. The study of UPC behavior provides further information on the basic grammar construction *strategies* of L2 learners, how feedback functions to aid gram-

mar construction, how it is utilized for this purpose and who provides such feedback. For example, it is widely accepted (Corder, 1967) that the basic grammar construction strategy used by learners is hypothesis testing. Within the error analysis literature, it is assumed that errors made by L2 learners are themselves indications of hypothesis testing. There is, however, no direct evidence for this from the study of errors which usually represent language data clean of all UPC performance phenomena. However, a study of UPC behavior shows that such strategies are *directly accessible* to study if performance data are studied.

4. There appears to exist a preference for a particular style of UPC behavior among L2 learners. Some learners seem to prefer certain kinds of speech behavior mechanisms over others. For example, it will be shown that one type of learner prefers to carefully plan his utterance internally and evidences such behavior in his speech with a predominance of silent and filled pauses while another type may exhibit little of the hesitation behavior and prefer to produce the utterance in whatever primitive form and work on perfecting the utterance after it has been produced. That is, some L2 learners appear to be primarily planners while others seem to be correctors.

Hesitation and speech correction behavior seems also to serve a complementary function to foreigner talk. Foreigner talk is a simplified system used by native speakers of a language in order to communicate with those perceived by them to be non-speakers of their language (Richards, 1974). However, in addition to simplifying the code on the part of native speakers to aid the non-native speaker in comprehending an utterance, there is probably a perceived need on the part of the non-native speaker to make himself understood with his limited L2 code. UPC behavior may contribute to this in various ways. That is, UPC probably serves a communicative function for the L2 learner in his contact with native speakers.

For example, one form of UPC behavior found with L2 learners is the use of rising intonation in English not to indicate a true yes/no question but rather to indicate some form of hypothesis testing. (In all of the examples below, E indicates experimenter, a native speaker, and S indicates subject, an L2 learner.)

1. E: How do you feel as a foreign student?
   S: Foreign student?[1]

Such a discourse device allows the L2 learner additional time to process the input from the native speaker who may or may not have taken into consideration that he is speaking to a non-native speaker. The rising intonation, as will be stated below, is used also to test hypotheses about the form of the input from the native speaker. The L2 learner is unsure of himself in such a context and therefore the rising intonation also indicates to the native speaker — foreign student? — i.e. Did I hear you correctly? In cases such as this the native speaker may not respond at all thus not disconfirming the L2 learner's hypothesis.

Another problem that L2 learners have in communicating with native speakers is that the interlanguage of L2 speakers contains much that is anomolous or strange to the native speaker. Hesitations, repetitions, false starts and overt word searching by the L2 learners act as clarification devices for the listener. In fact, when such behaviors are absent, L2 learner speech is difficult to understand. UPC behavior allows the native speaker to test out hypotheses about the deviant output of the learner. In short, certain kinds of UPC behavior of the L2 learner serve a communicative purpose beyond the planning and execution of his own utterance while, as we shall see, certain forms of this behavior can hinder communication.

Learner Style and UPC Behavior

It has been suggested above that certain types of UPC behavior appear to be related to other parameters of L2 learning behavior. Seliger and Gingras (1976) and Seliger (1977a, 1977c, 1978) have identified two types of L2 learners based on the degree of interaction and involvement with language learning environments. These two types, which are extremes on a continuum, were termed *High Input Generators* (HIG) and *Low Input Generators* (LIG) to refer to the amount of language input each engendered from other speakers. It was stated that the more input generated by the learner, the more likely would some of this input become intake to be used by the learner in the grammar construction process. HIGs were found to interact intensively with their target language environment both in and outside of language classes. It was found that these learners caused much more language data or input to be directed at them by initiating language interaction with others. In the series of studies noted above it was found that HIGs improved their own language proficiency to a significantly greater degree than did LIGs.

LIGs are those learners who avoid interacting with L2. In the language class, the typical LIG will respond only when called upon by the teacher and will avoid interacting with L2 speakers outside of the formal learning environment. His use of L2 is more or less limited to the classroom and to formal drill type responses rather than to communicative use of the language. The LIG as opposed to the HIG rarely takes the initiative in language interaction situations. In terms of learning and personality characteristics, the LIG was found to be more dependent on structured situations for learning and more insecure in situations which required experimenting with the language and likely to lead to the production of a possible error.

Given this distinction between HIGs and LIGs, one avenue of investigation is whether any differences in UPC style can be related to these two types of L2 learning style. That is, to what degree is UPC behavior also a function of the interaction and cognitive style characteristics of L2 learners?

That data reported here were collected from speech samples recorded during interviews between the researcher and adult intermediate level students of English as a second language in the Queens College English Language Institute, New York. The learners are from many different language backgrounds and all intend to pursue a full program of university study after completing the study of English. After the interviews were transcribed, the transcriptions were analyzed for UPC behavior. These subjects had already been classified in terms of HIG or LIG since they had participated in a previous study.

Findings

In general it was found that certain kinds of speech behavior were more prevalent with one type of learner than with another. For example, LIGs tended to use more measured speech. Their focus was definitely more on those aspects of UPC behavior which have been ascribed to the planning stage of speech rather than to the correction stage. This kind of speech was characterized by lots of silent pauses and filled pauses of the type /eh/ or /um:/. LIGs produced very few repeats of words, false starts or hypothesis testing questions such as appear in 1. above.

One subject in this study, a LIG, did not ask a single confirmatory or hypothesis testing question. Yet he attempted to answer the interviewer's questions even though it was obvious from his answer that he didn't fully understand. His answer, as will be seen below, consisted of words and phrases strung together and separated by pauses but which in total made little sense. Note, however, in the sample below, that there are no corrections, only one repeat, but lots of pauses. This subject was extremely careful about his utterance. Each phrase was carefully considered and formulated. The impression on the listener is one of labored conversation. While the speaker carefully works through his plan, the listener in such situations feels uncomfortable and often cannot restrain himself from attempting to predict what the speaker is trying to say and to interject such predictions.

2. E: What did you think about studying in the E.L.I. (English Language Institute) this semester? Was it good? Bad? How do you feel about it?

   S: As a result...on the whole...it good and eh...some...eh program is not connected together...because...I...without...eh, eh, critize (sic.) that critize (sic.) I um have a study and teach ten years uh uh program to teach...without any speciality (sic.) ...and sometimes in vocabulary especially...eh...teacher...eh do one hour eh give me vocabulary...eh and not practice this vocabulary. I find the word in the dictionary and waste my time borded (sic.).

Silent pauses in the segment above are indicated by (...). With this subject, the mean length of silent pauses was 1.1 seconds with a range of silent pauses of 0.6 seconds to 1.8 seconds. Filled pauses such as /uh/ or /eh/ had a mean length of approximately 1.07 seconds with a range of 0.4 seconds to 2.5 seconds.

There is almost no repetition in this kind of discourse, no paraphrasing and no overt word searching to give clues as to what the speaker intends. It is almost as tightly worded as a written passage if we remove the pauses. The burden of clarification is on the interlocutor who must continually ask clarifying questions of the L2 speaker to be certain that the message has been received correctly.

On the other hand, subjects who had been classified as HIG showed different kinds of speech behavior. HIGs tended to produce many more corrections and repeats and used hypothesis testing questions quite often. The effect was one of greater fluency in the sense that there was little silence. HIGs would often begin sentences before they had been completely planned out. Where LIGs' UPC behavior tended toward silent and filled pauses, HIGs developed different utterance planning strategies. They would lengthen a segment such as a vowel (indicated by :) as in:

3. S: I know:/ I know a different custom.

Or they paraphrased or did conscious word searching aloud as in:

4. S: Yes, very good circumstances is very beautiful. Very good uh sporting establishment and very big library and big ha:ll/ rest-/ cafeteria.

Note here that the subject has lengthened the vowel of the first word in the word search series.

Hypothesis testing questions, as noted previously, could be used as a discourse mechanism to gain time for planning. But note the use in the following exchange:

5. E: How did you feel as a foreign student at Queens College?
   S: My feel?
   E: Yes, how did you/ (subject interrupts at this point)
   S: Yes, very good etc. (continues with 4. above).

Note in this exchange that the subject does not really mean to ask a yes/no question, nor does it appear that she is simply stalling for time. It rather appears that this is a true instance of overt hypothesis testing. Her question focusses on one word of the input question - *feel*. E begins to repeat or paraphrase the question but is not allowed to complete his utterance. S interrupts and answers the original question.

In the following example, the learner combines word searching or lexical search, segment lengthening in the first lexeme in the series and rising intonation to indicate that overt hypothesis testing is being conducted:

6. S. (Responding to E's question about the curriculum)
So our teaching way is li:ne? /continue?/ no separate/
not isolating.

Here the learner lengthened a segment while planning or searching for a clearer formulation, followed this with two possible words for the concept but each was produced with an accompanying hypothesis testing intonation pattern and finally produced two more words each with falling intonation indicating that these were not being tested but rather were paraphrases of each other. An examination of the context in which this segment took place reveals that the subject was trying to express the idea of the integrativeness of the language lesson (i.e. reading, writing, speaking and listening are integrated and mutually reinforcing). Her thinking out loud almost provides a photograph of how the semantic information for the concept *integrated* is stored-

L2 Learner's Storage and Retrieval of the Concept "Integrated"

    line   (idea of linear relationship?)
    ↓
    continue   (idea of continuity?)
    ↓
    no separate (idea of things fitting together)
    ↓
    not isolating (idea of non-discreteness of language material)

Learners would also use the rising intonation but repeat the same word again as if they were confirming their own hypothesis. That is, once the word was uttered for inspection and found acceptable, it was repeated a second time with falling intonation to indicate its acceptability. In 7A below, it appears that while the word was uttered with normal intonation in the first instance, it may have sounded strange to the speaker and was repeated with rising intonation the second time. In this case, it is possible that the learner wanted the confirmation of the interlocutor.

7.A. S: I very embarrassed/ embarrassed?
  B. S: I/I understand/ I understand.
  C. S: I like conversation?/ conversation time.

In these examples, the hypothesis testing and clarification appear to involve only the speaker / learner. However, in the discourse below, the interviewer and the learner are involved. Note also how the conversation digresses into clarifying something not related to the original problem in the discourse.

8. S: I have to be /preyšənt/ when I contact with somebody.
   E: You have to be...?
   S: I have to be?
   E: Yes, what did you say? To be...

S: I have to be...
E: Pleasant? What did you say?
S: Patient. (S produces a perfect pronunciation of the originally intended word with apparent ease.)

Segmental Lengthening

While it is possible to lengthen any language sound marked +continuant, in the examples found in the data for L2 learners, it was common to lengthen vowels rather than consonants. Why, for example, would the speaker lengthen the vowel of the second syllable of *begin* in number 10 below rather than the final consonant? Segmental lengthening appears to serve the same function that silent or filled pauses do - notably, time to plan or inspect the utterance. Sometimes, as will be seen below, as a result of the hesitation provided by the segment lengthening, the speaker will completely retrace his utterance and change it. In other instances, the lenghtened segment will be followed by a repetition of that part of the utterance containing the lengthened segment.

However, in this instance, the speaker begins his utterance again but with noticeably increased speed and apparent confidence. Because of this change of speed, it is possible to conceive of the segment lengthening as not only a planning strategy but also as a hypothesis testing strategy. The lengthened segment may serve the function of allowing the speaker to inspect the hypothesized utterance internally while holding open the line of communication ("holding the floor" so to speak). The increased speed following the lengthened segment may therefore indicate that the utterance has been inspected and found acceptable.

9. Vowel Lengthening and Repetition
    S: We have/ we have three::/ three laboratories.
    (Double :: indicates especially long holding of vowel.)
    S: All of:/ all of our classes.

10. Vowel Lengthening with Incomplete Word
    S: uh, begi:/ begin to quarrel.

11. Vowel Lengthening, Filled Pause and Repetition
    S: We have uh/ we have uh/ we: ha::ve uh: vocabulary.
    (Obvious word searching was going on here. The last word in the utterance was said quickly once it was found.)

Maclay and Osgood (1959) in their study of hesitation and correction behavior in the speech of native speakers found that after all correction and repetition, the speaker returned and executed the whole constituent. In the current study, one of the L2 subjects produced the following utterance:

12. Vowel Lengthening and Repetition of Constituent

    S: We talk abou:t/ about her lessons.

Note that the speaker returned to the beginning of the prepositional phrase. He did not produce something like:

    12.A. *S: We talk abou:t/ her lessons.

Such behavior would indicate that the learner has at least acquired an internal representation of the constituent boundaries of English. Whether such constituent boundary behavior is transferred cross-linguistically from the learner's L1 is a matter of further research.

Since, as stated above, it was suggested that lengthening can serve as a device for the inspection of the utterance plan, it might be expected that lengthening might be followed by a complete reformulation of the utterance. Such an example of L2 learner UPC behavior was found in the following:

    13. S: Because four tea:/ we have four teachers.

Several studies concerned with errors produced by L2 learners have dealt with avoidance strategy (Schachter, 1974; Kleinmann, 1977; Seliger, 1977b). Avoidance strategy refers to the L2 learner's avoiding the use of forms with which he feels unconfident or which, for reasons revealed by contrastive analysis, are different in various ways from the form of his own language. In 13. above, it is obvious that the speaker has decided to reform his utterance and to avoid the clause beginning with *because*. S begins the utterance but apparently is covertly scanning the utterance plan. Realizing that he cannot produce this syntactic form, he retraces to begin again. Such avoidance and retracing is not uncommon with native speakers of a language when they realize that an utterance may be misunderstood or awkward to produce.

Interference in Utterance Planning and Correction Behavior

If, as postulated here, the performance data of speech can be used as an indication of the underlying hypothesis testing strategies and evidence for the psychological nature of learner's grammar, the speech correction behavior of one of the subjects in this study provides interesting evidence with regard to the storage of lexicon and the way language responses may be triggered by seemingly superficial and non-meaningful cues.

The subject who supplied the interference data is a speaker of Haitian, Creole and French. She had been classified as a High Input Generator. Again, as with other HIGs, while her speech contained many corrections and repeats, it contained little of the silent or filled pauses which were most common in the speech of the Low Input Generator. Her strategy, as with the other HIGs, was to first produce the utterance and then work on it. In our short conversation, she produced three utterances which contained examples of lexical interference from French. Whatever utterance control this subject was employing did not apparently work until after production. In two cases the interference appears to have been triggered by something in the speaker's own utterance. In the third case, it simply appears that the French word was more easily accessible. What is interesting in all of these cases is that we are not dealing with a case of code-switching as it is normally understood since the speaker knew that the interlocutor did not know French. Assuming that the goal of a speaker is to make himself understood, it is likely that the speaker would realize consciously that the use of French would be inappropriate in this particular context.

In the first example, the phonetic similarity of two English words in the subject's own grammatically incorrect utterance to a French word, triggered a French response which was quickly corrected:

14. E: How old are you?
    S: How old am me? eh ventrois/ oh, twenty-three.

Two possible explanations which can be given for this speech error: 1) The sound of *am* plus *me* blended together sound like the French *ami* which while semantically irrelevant to this exchange triggered some code-switching mechanism leading to the retrieval of *ventrois* instead of *twenty-three*. 2) A second possible explanation is that numbers or the automatic information such as giving one's age might be more readily accessible in French for this subject. In any event, this kind of error might be taken as proof of some kind of compound storage system. The essential question would be where in the chain of events of utterance planning would such an error occur. Since explanation 1) requires the absence of semantic information, it might be assumed that there is a possibility for phonetic interference as the trigger which then sends the utterance plan back to the semantic and lexical level. (See Seliger, 1979 for a further analysis of the utterance plan in second language speech errors.)

The next error also appears to have been triggered by a phonetic cue. In this instance it is the similarity between the target language word and the first language word both of which are derived from a common semantic source.

15. S: Twice a month, every fifteen days, but not duf/two/two/twice on the week.

In the repetition series, the first morpheme is heard on the tape quite clearly as /duf/. The French for *twice*, the target of the speaker, is /dufwa/. The similarity between the first consonant and vowel in the English and French caused the error. The semantic source of both the English and the French word is the concept of *two*. Instead, the phonetic similarity led first to the French word for *twice*. When the speaker began to produce this, she realized her mistake and went back to the original source *two* and then produced the correct word at the end of the series. What is interesting here, is that this speaker correctly used *twice* at the beginning of her utterance.

FIGURE 1

Possible lexical Storage System of French-speaking English Learner as Evidenced by Speech Error

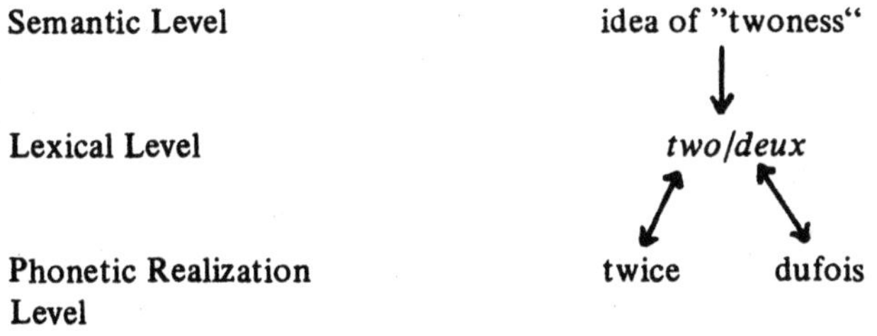

Semantic Level	idea of "twoness"
	↓
Lexical Level	*two/deux*
	↙ ↘
Phonetic Realization Level	twice dufois

Because of compound storage, phonetic similarity of *two* to *dufois* and *deux* could trigger a French response in an English environment.

The third interference error shows that in some cases the L1 word was more readily retrievable. This in itself is not surprising in the case of L2 learners. However it does show that while the plan may be formulated in L2, this does not necessarily prevent reference to the L1 word store for some learners. It is unusual in the sense that it would be expected that the syntactic frame would create a cognitive set for L2 and that while errors might occur at more abstract levels, the speaker would not normally mix L2 and L1 components together in one sentence unless we are truely dealing with a compound system.

16. S: I not have any/ I not have nobody ami/ nobody friends.

Two interesting things occur in this utterance: First the speaker begins the utterance correctly observing the rule for negative used with *any*. Once the lexical search begins, the focus is shifted away from the syntactic rule and we find the speaker producing a double negative as well as the French word for the target item. The speaker corrects the French word with an English word by retracing the entire phrase but retaining the double negative. Again this error may be interpreted as demonstrating that this speaker has stored the lexicon in a compound system.

Conclusion

This study has shown that an important source of data which reveals the cognitive strategies of L2 learners exists in actual speech performance. Much as slips of the tongue (Fromkin, 1971, 1973) reveal our underlying phonological processes, so too can utterance planning and correction behavior provide direct empirical evidence of the psychological reality of utterance planning and hypothesis testing strategies used by second language learners.

Previous evidence for hypothesis testing as a basic second language acquisition strategy has depended on indirect or implied evidence which viewed the error alone as proof of the existence of covert hypothesis testing. The problem with viewing errors, which are competence based, as opposed to mistakes, lapses and speech corrections, which are supposedly performance based, as proof of the existence of hypothesis testing as a basic language acquisition process or strategy, is that one never sees the process itself but only its product. It is then difficult to distinguish output which may be the product of hypothesis testing from output which, though deviant from the target grammar, may still be the output of a stable rule in the grammar of the learner which is no longer undergoing change. The evidence from UPC behavior provides tangible proof that such processes are indeed going on and part of the construction of the L2 learner's grammar.

Finally, the data of this study indicate that some learners prefer careful planning with little testing or experimentation evident in actual speech while others clearly tend toward overt trial and error and correction of utterances during the actual act of speech. The latter group have also been found in other studies (Seliger, 1977a) to be more successful language learners and more active participants in the language learning environment. Their preference for certain types of speech behavior may indicate that they are more involved in the language learning process. This may help to explain why they are more successful in the long run than the more passive learner dependent on covert utterance planning.

REFERENCES

CORDER, S.P. 1967. The Significance of Learner's Errors. *International Review of Applied Linguistics.* 5, 161-170.

FROMKIN, V.A. 1971. The Non-Anomalous Nature of Anomalous Utterances. *Language.* 47, 27-52.

FROMKIN, V.A. (ed.) 1973. *Speech Errors as Linguistic Evidence.* The Hague: Mouton.

GARRET, M.F. 1975. The Analysis of Sentence Production. In: G.H. Bower (ed.). *The Psychology of Learning and Motivation.* Vol. 9. New York: Academic Press, 133-177.

GOLDMAN-EISLER, F. 1968. *Psycholinguistics: Experiments in Spontaneous Speech.* London, New York: Academic Press.

KLEINMANN, H. 1977. Avoidance Behavior in Adult Second Language Acquisition. *Language Learning.* 27, 93-107.

MACLAY, H. and C.E.. Osgood. 1959. Hesitation Phenomena in Spontaneous English Speech. *Word.* 15, 19-44.

MILLER, G. 1966. Language and Psychology. In: E.H. Lenneberg (ed.). *New Directions in the Study of Language.* Cambridge, Mass.: MIT Press, 89-107.

RICHARDS, J.C. 1974. Social Factors, Interlanguage and Language Learning. In: J.C. Richards (ed.). *Error Analysis: Perspectives on Second Language Acquisition.* London: Longman, 64-91.

SCHACHTER, J. 1974. An Error in Error Analysis. *Language Learning.* 24, 205-214.

SELIGER, H.W. 1977a. Does Practice Make Perfect?: A Study of Interaction Patterns and L2 Competence. *Language Learning.* 27, 263-278.

SELIGER, H.W. 1977b. Semantic Presuppositions Underlying Avoidance Strategy. *C.U.N.Y. Forum Papers in Linguistics.* Fall, 3, 63-83.

SELIGER, H.W. 1977c. A Study of Interaction Patterns and L2 Competence. In: C.A. Henning (ed.). *Proceedings of the Los Angeles Second Language Research Forum*, U.C.L.A., 118-131.

SELIGER, H.W. 1978. On the Evolution of Error Type. *Indian Journal of Applied Linguistics* (in press).

SELIGER, H.W. 1979. The Significance of Learners' Mistakes: Theoretical Issues in the Study of L2 Acquisition (in press).

SELIGER, H.W. and R. Gingras. 1976. Who Speaks How Much and to Whom? A Study of Interaction Patterns in Second Language Classromms. Unpublished Paper presented at the Colloquium on Verbal and Non-Verbal Behavior in Second Language Learning. National TESOL Convention, New York.

CONTEXTUAL HYPOTHESIS-TESTING-PROCEDURES IN SPEECH PRODUCTION [1]

Hans W. Dechert
University of Kassel

Problem

The acquisition of language is essentially a form of cognitive learning. Cognitive learning is understood as the learner's spontaneous and creative application (Chomsky, 1964; Dulay and Burt, 1974a,b) of his learning procedures leading to an individual interlanguage system in L 1 as well as between L 1 and L 2 (Cooper, 1970; Corder, 1971, 1974, 1975b; Dickerson, 1975; Dulay and Burt, 1972; Erdmann, 1973; Ervin-Tripp, 1973, 1974; Ferguson, 1971, 1975; James, 1971; Nemser, 1971; Richards, 1971a,b, 1972; Schumann, 1974, 1976; Selinker, 1969, 1971, 1972, 1975; Slama-Cazacu, 1971; Tarone, 1976; Taylor, 1974).

Five major processes constituting interlanguage systems have been proposed to be central to second language acquisition: language transfer; transfer-of-training; strategies of second-language learning; strategies of second-language communication; overgeneralization of TL linguistic material (Selinker, 1969, 1971, 1972). In their 1975 paper Selinker, Swain and Dumas have added to this list the strategy of simplification of the TL system as a special form of overgeneralization or a "superordinate strategy with overgeneralization and language transfer as types of simplifications."

This hypothesis, however, as Adjemian (1976) has stated, fails to explain certain IL-phenomena. He has introduced the concept of 'permeability' and loss of permeability as a special characteristic feature of IL into the IL-discussion. Interestingly enough, he has also mentioned the Hypothesis-testing construct in the same paper. It seems to me that the linguistic descriptions of certain IL-phenomena given by Selinker, Swain and Dumas add little to a psycholinguistic or psychological understanding of the individual learner's acquisition of his IL.

This process of acquiring an IL may be regarded as a specific form of Hypothesis-Testing (HT). This notion, relating to the acquisition of language by children,

---

[1] The original document was read at the 5th International Congress of Applied Linguistics, August, 1978, Montreal. An abstract appeared in Language and Language Behavior Abstracts and a microfiche of the paper as read at the Congress is available from Sociofiche P.O. Box 22206, San Diego, CA. 92122, U.S.A. for $ 3. on a prepaid basis only.

partially goes back to Roger Brown's 'Creative-Construction Hypothesis' (Dulay and Burt, 1974a) and, of course, more closely, to Chomsky (1959, 1964). In Jerrold Katz's words, "according to Chomsky's conception, the child" when learning the syntax of his primary language "formulates hypotheses about the rules of the linguistic description of the language whose sentences he is hearing, derives predictions from such hypotheses about the linguistic structures of sentences he will hear in the future, checks these predictions against the new sentences he encounters, eliminates those hypotheses that are contrary to the evidence, and evaluates those that are not eliminated by a simplicity principle which selects the simplest as the best hypothesis concerning the rules underlying the sentences he has heard and will hear. This process of hypothesis construction, verification, and evaluation repeats itself until the child matures past the point where the language acquisition device operates" (Katz, 1966).

Thus the HT-construct, to be sure, in its initial stage of discussion refers to perception only and tries to explain the acquisition of syntax during the child's development in his primary language as a constructive process on the basis of the sentences heard.

This construct of HT has been strongly criticized by Martin D.S. Braine (1971). Since the phrase 'Contextual Hypothesis-Testing' in my topic is supposed to allude to Braine's concept of 'Contextual Generalization' in verbal learning (1963) and since his criticism of the HT-construct is still considered to be a very substantial one (McLaughlin, 1978), I must comment briefly on that.

With special reference to the HT-Construct in concept attainment, (Bruner, Goodnow and Austin, 1956) Braine has denied that such a model can explain the natural acquisition of grammar among children, as a child under normal circumstances is not told what is and what is not an instance of what is to be learned, as in the case of concept attainment tasks through HT after each trial. Language learning, such as concept attainment, he claims, depends on the feedback provided. This feedback is the learner's only means of discovering the true hypothesis. If there is no alternative situation in which correct sentences can be tested to be correct and incorrect ones to be incorrect, one cannot transfer the HT-construct to natural language acquisition. As the child's verbal input mainly consists of the sentences he hears and not the sentences he doesn't hear, the HT-construct seems to be irrelevant to language learning.

Braine's argument is based on the assumption that a child learning his language according to the HT-construct needs immediate and continuous feedback in order to test and thus learn what is reinforced to be correct.

The findings of Marvin Levine and his associates (1975), especially on the equivalence of positive reinforcement and nonreinforcement leading to the Blank-Trials-Law in concept attainment, do not only refute Braine's assumption on the necessity of feedback in concept attainment, but also give rise to some doubts as to the validity of the same argument referring to language acquisition.

Moreover, the examples of children's utterances given by Braine do not prove what they are supposed to, but reveal only that children during certain stages of their cognitive and linguistic development hold certain linguistic hypotheses even if they are not reinforced or are corrected by their parents, as long as they get along with them. The fact that their parents correct the utterances obviously indicates that communication has taken place, that they have been able to get the message across with a very limited repertoire of hypotheses.

This kind of hypothesis construction and testing doesn't seem to be very much different from the procedures of second language learners whose IL-grammar and incidental 'backslidings' are deficient all over but who are successful in the way that they are understood so that there is no need to correct 'false' hypotheses.

This is to say that HT may not only occur in the perception of language during a child's acquisition of syntax — as Chomsky and Katz have hypothesized — but as our data seem to indicate, even more so, in the production of speech far beyond early developmental stages during childhood. I would assume that the flexibility and fluency of advanced adult language learners depend on their ability to maintain and develop linguistic hypotheses or guesses or, as S.C. Pepper (1948) has put it, 'hunches'.

In using the term HT in a somewhat broader sense, I am making the following assumptions

— Adult second language learners have a set of L 1, L 2 and IL-hypotheses available.

— Lexical search seems to be much more the concern of an adult second language speaker than grammatical correctness (Schlue, 1977).

— Distinct speech productions of a second language learner reflect certain unique stages of his individual language learning process.

— If these productions are 'erroneous' they are likely to disclose either a complete lack of correct hypotheses or a competition of speech plans, i.e. of contradicting hypotheses in the state of being tested against each other.

— As Krashen has proposed (1975), there must be an evaluative monitoring of the testing of linguistic hypotheses which is responsible for the final decision for one of them. It does not depend on feedback or reinforcement, but rather reflects 'insight' into what is correct.

— There must be something like a perceptual/productive cycle of verbal information processing that is context-dependent and context-producing at the same time.

The term 'contextual' in the phrase 'Contextual HT' in my topic, as opposed to 'associative', stands for the assumption that the corpus I am dealing with in this paper represents natural speech in which events are t h e structuring principle. That is to say that the whole of the stories toid, is considered to be the overall unit of production, its subunits — I have called them episodic units — represent the event structure of the whole.

It is further understood that, generally speaking, there exists a contextual organization of memory from which linguistic hypotheses and schemata are retrieved. It is this structural organization that is held to be responsible for the construction of the texts. The correctness of the linguistic hypotheses to be tested in the process of speech production lies in their appropriateness to the context to be verbalized, in their context dependency. The total event of the stories as a whole and the semantic network constituting it as well as the episodic units embedded into it make up this context. An analysis of this contextual structure as a means of assessing the procedures and problems of the linguistic construction process must be a holistic one.

'Contextual' also stands for the interaction of the story teller with his past and present experience, with his world which he brings into his task. It is the pre-existing knowledge of the world, his 'World Hypotheses' (Pepper), that is the structural principle of the texts. This knowledge has been called in the Bartlett-tradition (Bartlett, 1932) a 'schema'. The schemata a story-teller chooses make him 'contextualize' his experience into a unique, never before and never again ocurring text (Jenkins, 1977; Kintsch, 1970, 1977; Kintsch and Kozminski, 1977; Mandler and Johnson, 1977).

There are, of course, other connotations to the term 'contextual', other personal variables concerning the story-teller (his educational background, his linguistic competence, the kind of material he has studied, etc.), variables concerning the type of story, the kind of elicitation task, the situation of recording, and so forth. They certainly have some influence but are considered of minor importance for us.

Although I also do not deny that a 'contextualist' approach to speech production has sociological and sociolinguistic implications, the concerns of this paper are centred upon cognition. For this reason I do not deal with problems such as the dialect determinants of our speech samples.

The HT-construct developed so far, however, leaves two decisive questions unanswered:

- Under what circumstances does an adult speaker of a first or second language test alternative hypotheses as to their appropriateness since there is obviously a lot of speaking running smoothly with few or no conflicting passages involved?
- If hypotheses are tested from what set or memory store are they taken and what organization of memory may be responsible for the construction of competing linguistic hypotheses?

It may well be that the processing of speech in the second language as well as in the primary one is such a complex and difficult procedure that it can't possibly be done without the occurrence of planning difficulties and the implicit or explicit choice between alternatives, as our analysis of David Crystal's corpus has shown (cf. Deese, 1978).

There can be no doubt that many search problems in the concrete speech planning process are due to a sudden inaccessibility, but not general inavailability of the verbal information needed. To a certain extent, in other words, search processes in speech production and the testing of alternative hypotheses are caused by a lack of the relevant cues (Tulving and Pearlstone, 1966).

Procedure

In a number of case studies with male and female German university students of English and male and female American and English exchange students of German (until Juli 1977 : N=8) in the Department of Modern Languages at Kassel University, samples of L 1 and L 2 free speech productions have been recorded, transcribed, and analysed over a period of eight months.

At the same time an English corpus with interviews and discussions of male and female native speakers of English with different backgrounds in various contexts (Crystal and Davy, 1975) has been analysed to get additional information about the speech of native English speakers.

The occurring extralinguistic phenomena in these speech samples such as pauses, slips of the tongue, false starts, repeats, repairs and intonation contours have been taken as indicators of speech planning procedures (Fromkin, 1971, 1973; Garrett, 1975, 1976).

Subject

The recordings of Barbara — a Kassel English major — were made in December 1976. At that time she was 23 years old. In 1977 she passed her final examination with above average grades and is now a teacher of English. In 1976 she had had 8 years of English in high school (Gymnasium) and 4 years of language teaching by native speakers of English in Kassel University. Some time before the recording she had spent about half a year in a Midwestern College in the US as an exchange student. Her social and educational background as well as her exposure to the English language is high above average.

Collection of Speech Sample

Before and during the recording, done by a fellow student whom she knew well, we tried to create a relaxed situation. There were no time constraints. She would stop and relax and chat in between the recordings as long as she wanted. Nobody else was present.

Method of Elicitation

The cartoons taken from Goldman-Eisler (1961), among other material such as collages on various topics, were presented in printed form of about 15 x 20 cm for each picture, with all pictures making up one story being presented together. No additional verbal information or explanation — except the items in the cartoons themselves — was given to avoid any intrusions that might have influenced the organization of the texts.

She was told that we wanted to find out how well an advanced German student would do on an elicitation task of that sort and that she should try to reproduce the story verbally at normal speed after having carefully looked at the set of pictures.

Transcriptions and Analysis

The recordings were then transcribed by 3 student assistants indepedently. The resulting transcriptions were compared with each other and with the recordings, obvious omissions and mistakes were corrected.

To get sound data on the speech-pause-intonation patterns of the speech samples the recordings were analysed with a Frøkjaer-Jensen Fundamental-Frequency-Meter Type FFM 650 and a 4-channel Siemens Oscillomink L. The exact speech-pause distribution in the production of the speech sample can be taken from the graphic display of channel 2 and 3; the intonation contour from the display of channel 4. The transcripts were then compared with the results of the instrumental analysis, in cases of disagreement, with the recordings again and then corrected.

As I have shown elsewhere (Dechert, forthcoming) this combined aural and instrumental analysis, taking pausal and intonation patterns as two decisive factors in the assessment of the inherent units of speech production, leads to the construct of episodic unit of processing. These units are characterized by pauses and falling pitch before and after them. All (or almost all) repairs of false starts, slips of the tongue, repeats etc. take place within their boundary lines. They are also characterized by a lot of other features such as opening and closing signals, theme, narrative function, event structure, tense, etc.

There are structural subschemata in constructing a story which, in the case of second language learners, at least on an advanced level and with two culturally closely related languages such as English and German, are probably transferred from the primary language.

The boundary lines between these units were the guiding principle in finally structuring the 4 texts (Appendix I. 1-4).

The pauses occurring at various points within the boundary lines of the episodic units are considered to be indicators of verbal planning and competition of different plans of processing. In connection with the false starts, slips-of-the-tongue, repeats and repairs they disclose slots in the overall schemata where verbal planning on a sublevel type can be assessed.

Analysis of Data

The Texts 1-4 in Appendix I illustrate our method of analysing and transcribing speech. The intended ideal versions as the result of HT are printed in capital letters, the rejected hypotheses in small ones.

These texts show

— that the search processes (indicated by pauses, slips of the tongue, repetitions, prolongations, repairs, etc.) occurring in producing them are accompanied by a steady monitoring;

— that in the process of their production it is mainly lexical search that is causing the disruptions and hesitations (besides some problems in syntactic planning as in 2.2.1 and 4.5.1).

The following hermeneutic interpretation of the data is thus restricted to a more general delineation of HT-procedures in the first three texts and a closer elaboration of three lexical search procedures revealed through the slots in lines 4.2.1, 4.2.2, and 4.4.1 of Text 4.

The Corpus

Texts 1-3 (Appendix I)

In line 1.3.1 there is a remarkable number of disruptions and pauses disclosing a search process for expressing the right word for that "thing" that bears the theme "Nude" in the picture. Is it the word "shield" (resembling the German L 1 expression "Schild") is it tag, label, plate, badge, sign, inscription, caption, ...?

1.3.1 BUT SUDDENLY . HE – CATCHES . SIGHT – OF – A TITLE . . .

The decision for "TITLE" as the result of an avoidance strategy and a search process, obviously based on the underlying L 1 expression "Titel", only comes close to L 2 competence such as the phrase CATCHES SIGHT OF in this context, thus giving a fine example of IL speech production.

In the following line Barbara is having a similar problem

3.5.1 BUT IN THE MIDDLE – OF THE STREET . *THE* . SIGN CHANGES ...

What is it that changes, the whole thing: the traffic light? Or part of it, and if so, what is it called? Is it a technical term or a more general word?
Her decision for "SIGN" shows the latter tendency.

Lines 2.2.1 to 2.3.1 reveal an interesting complex of competitive planning and HT.

The verbal information given in all three pictures of this cartoon is "Wishing Well" on top of the roof covering the well. So there is really no reason why Barbara should have trouble to just read

2.2.1 I WAS WONDERING IF THIS WISHING WELL ...

But she doesn't, she hesitates, it takes more than five seconds to come to the decision "THIS WELL". Has she had trouble calling a WISHING WELL a WELL because she tries to avoid repetion of WISHING WELL for reasons of variation of style? Or for classificatory reasons in connection with her mental lexicon? Or is she already dealing with quite another problem, indicated by the following subphonemic slip of the tongue "p" in

2.2.2 wishes – p [ut] my wish MY WISHES ...?

Perhaps she is already looking at and considering the second picture and on the lexical search for the right word expressing "what is done with the coin" and about to decide between "put" and "THREW". At the same time she can't avoid working on a semantic problem not yet solved, a highly contextual one: is it one wish or more wishes she is having, right now, when saying so? Or do wishing wells fulfill just one wish (the one she has in mind concerning her husband's beard) or wishes in general?

It is probably this particular 'stress' of several speech plans to be handled with at the same time – or almost the same time – that causes Barbara to 'slide into' the error "throw" for "THREW", additionally enforced by the fact that "put" has only one form for past and present, within a clear piece of narration in the past.

In 3.2.1 we find another example for a subphonemic slip disclosing a planning problem that results from lexical search (and possibly from a sudden inaccessibility of the English word):

3.2.1 AFTER A WHILE HE HAS TO CROSS . THE s . STREET ON A PEDESTRIAN CROSSING – / /

Most likely it is the rather special technical term PEDESTRIAN CROSSING she is looking for. As soon as she has found it she makes the decision for "TO CROSS THE STREET ON A PEDESTRIAN CROSSING" against "to cross the street", which would have been correct. For contextual reasons the version PEDESTRIAN CROSSING seems to be superior because this crossing plays an important role in the imagery of the whole story. On the other hand it is this L 1 dependent image ("... die Straße auf einem Zebrastreifen überqueren ...") which causes her to choose ON instead of "at".

These examples taken from the first 3 texts may suffice to exemplify some of the monitoring and HT-procedures in Barbara's corpus.

Text 4 (Appendix I. 4. a,b,c)

Everybody starting out to tell a story has to make certain decisions in advance to set up a frame of reference as a sort of outline for the following narration.

Some of the decisions having been made by Barbara before the construction of Text 4 obviously are:

— She uses the past and sticks to it.
— She uses a chronological order of events.
— She chooses a particular perspective: she plays the role of the narrator and the main female character in one person as in Text 2.
— She leaves the end of the story open without a resolution.
— She applies an avoidance strategy since she evidently misses the point by not grasping the theme "conversation piece" in picture 1. In missing the irony of the story she has a special problem: to construct it with a somewhat different theme in mind.

Since for the present purpose it does not seem necessary to give an elaborate analysis of the whole text, I have chosen the exposition (lines 4.1.1 to 4.4.2). This is also justified by recent findings (Kintsch and Kozminsky, 1977) which have shown that there is sort of a primacy effect in the reproduction of stories as the exposition mostly turns out to be the most elaborate and carefully planned part of it.

The narrative structure of Barbara's exposition of Text 4 is given in Appendix I. 4.b. It deals with the episodic units (U) 1 to 4. This analysis shows a very careful and minute structure, comprising a General Setting, a Detailed Setting, and the Expository Event, with various subcategories and subunits. This narrative structure is not identical with the schema of the exposition given in Appendix I. 4.c that reflects the actual processing plan and different overlapping speech plans in competition.

The first sentence of the story

4.1.1 ONE AFTERNOON I WENT OUT SHOPPING

introduces in a very general way the time, action and location of the incident. This sentence is Barbara's invention; it does not have an equivalent in the first picture of the cartoon series. But it presents a narrative problem: in the first scene of the cartoon the lady is standing before the window looking at the lamp, in Barbara's first sentence she is walking, and she continues to walk as the slip "w"

4.2.1 PASSING . SEVERAL SHOPS . *I w*[ent] eh . . .

within the semantic field I WENT OUT demonstrates. As the pauses additionally show, the narrator gets mixed up with two different contexts and plans: the one suggested by the first picture of the cartoon and the one introduced with the first sentence. The lady in front of the story must be stopped. She does so, but another problem comes up at once

4.2.1 STOPPED – – – on a shop *where* vs.

4.2.2 AT A SHOP *WHERE*

Again it seems to be the complexity of speech plans in competition that allows an IL-error "on" (for German "an") instead of "in front of", "before" to 'slide in'. And once more this is only part of the complexity, as the prolongations *"where"* and *"WHERE"* show. The hypothesis that "antiques are sold there" vs. the hypothesis that "antiques can be bought there" obviously are tested against each other before the final version

4.2.2 *WHERE* – ANTIQUES COULD BE . BOUGHT

is found probably relating to the semantic network BUY – BOUGHT (4.3.2; 4.4.2; 4.6.2) for further contextual reasons.

Whereas the testing of "pane" against "WINDOW" in line 4.3.1 with the repetition and false decision for "pane" seems to be of minor interest, the slot in

4.4.1 it wasn't [expensive] vs. IT WAS QUITE EXPENSIVE

unfolds a very interesting type of context-dependent planning not mentioned so far.

This phrase is preceded by the lady's fatal decision to buy the conversation piece. Being displayed in the antique shop, it is not likely to be a cheap piece of junk. But the narrator who has completely taken the role of the lady knows this decision will soon have its aftereffect: the conversation piece will be the cause of the disruption of the conversation with her husband when she comes home. What other excuse should she have than but to say: it was an occasion, it was a good buy, it was inexpensive, you should be delighted, too, my dear! But Barbara turns down this version and rephrases it to "IT WAS QUITE EXPENSIVE" thus leaving it ambiguous, still capable of saying "although it was quite expensive, it was a good buy", but also changing the perspective from the future excuses and rationalizations of the wife in the fight with her husband to a more objective consideration of the true function of the lamp in the context of the whole text. For that reason it got to be an expensive antique piece, a conversation piece that concludes the conversation. Although Barbara somewhat misses this point — the uncertainty whether it is an expensive or inexpensive lamp may also be an expression of that — she finally manages to choose the adequate hypothesis from a contextual point of view. This kind of HT seems to be a very complex one reflecting a type of cultural competence of a metalinguistic type relevant in both languages she speaks.

Result

Speech production procedures depend to a large extent on the context of the elicitation task (or context of the interview or discussion) and the availability and accessibility of relevant linguistic hypotheses in the speaker to cope with this task. These procedures are likely to be successful if the speaker's past and present experience of events lends him support for a holistic analysis and a comprehension of the task. If he is able to structure and restructure the task's context — even if he misinterprets it — he is capable of setting up a frame of reference for the further testing of various other linguistic hypotheses on lower levels.

Conclusion

The construct of HT in discrimination learning in general, the construct of the holistic reception strategy in concept attainment, and the contextualist approach to human information retrieval provide a potential theoretical explanation of various phenomena occurring in the production of speech by second language speakers.

This construct needs further elaboration and discussion. Its consequences for the reconsideration of language acquisition depending on the individual learner's specific hypothetical grasp of the context to be verbalized seem to be evident.

Appendix I

KEY TO SYMBOLS

Pauses:

(.)	0.2 – 0.5 seconds
(–)	0.6 – 1.0 seconds
(– –)	1.1 – 1.5 seconds
(– – –)	1.6 – 2.0 seconds
(– – – –)	2.1 – 2.5 seconds
(– – – – –)	2.6 seconds and longer
eh	Filled Pause
AND	Prolongation
/ /	Unit Boundary Line
S	Scene in the Cartoons
U	Episodic Unit
L	Location of Action
P	Perspective of Narration
R	Report
M	Interior Monologue

Text 1

1.1.1 A MAN VISITS A MUSEUM OF MODERN ARTS – //

1.2.1 HE PASSES THE SCULPTURES – – – eh . AND HE DOESN'T GIVE *THEM* – – – ANY GLANCE
1.2.2 BECAUSE THEY DON'T INTEREST HIM . AT ALL – //

1.3.1 BUT SUDDENLY . HE – CATCHES . SIGHT – OF – A TITLE UNDER ONE SCULPTURE . //

1.4.1 THE TITLE IS NUDE – – //

1.5.1 THIS INTERESTS HIM – / *AND* – – *HE* . STOPS AND TRIES *TO* – – FIND – –
1.5.2 THE NUDITY – IN THE SCULPTURE . //

Text 2

2.1.1 MY HUSBAND AN I ONCE . APPROACHED A WISHING WELL – – – //

2.2.1 I wondered – I WAS WONDERING IF *THIS* – – – he . WELL . COULD REALLY FULFILL
2.2.2 wishes – p my wish MY WISHES . //

2.3.1 SO . I put a . I throw . THREW A COIN . INTO THE WELL – AND MADE A WISH – – – – //

2.4.1 SUDDENLY – MY HUSBAND – – – LOOKED QUITE PUZZLLED – AND SURPRISED – –
2.4.2 *BECAUSE* – – MY WISH – – HAD BECOME TRUE – //

2.5.1 HE HAD NO LONGER A LONG BEARD – ONLY HIS MOUSTACHE WAS LEFT //

Text 3

3.1.1 A MAN WALKS ALONG A SIDE WALK – – – //
3.2.1 AFTER A WHILE HE HAS TO CROSS . THE s . STREET ON A PEDESTRIAN CROSSING – //
3.3.1 THERE IS A – eh . TRAFFIC LIGHT . WHICH SAYS WALK . //
3.4.1 AND *SO* – HE WALKS – *AND* . TRIES TO CROSS THE STREET – //
3.5.1 BUT IN THE MIDDLE – OF THE STREET . *THE* . SIGN CHANGES TO DON'T WALK – – //
3.6.1 THE MAN . OBEYS THE SIGN AND JUST STOPS //

Appendix I. 4. a

Text 4

4.1.1 ONE AFTERNOON I WENT OUT SHOPPING – //

4.2.1 PASSING . SEVERAL SHOPS . *I* w eh . STOPPED – – – on a shop *where* .
4.2.2 AT A SHOP *WHERE* – ANTIQUES COULD BE . BOUGHT – – – – //

4.3.1 I SAW A BEAUTIFUL LAMP STANDING . IN THE – pane – WINDOW . pane .
4.3.2 *an* – – *AND* – – DECIDED TO BUY IT – – – //

4.4.1 it wasn't IT WAS QUITE EXPENSIVE – – BUT I LIKED IT SO MUCH
4.4.2 AND SO I I JUST BOUGHT IT – //

4.5.1 AT HOME – *I* – SHOWED IT – TO MY HUSBAND – – AND THOUGHT – –
4.5.2 *HE* . TOO WOULD BE VERY . DELIGHTED – TO SEE SUCH A . CUTE LAMP – //

4.6.1 BUT – HE LOOKED VERY – – SHOCKED WHEN HE SAW IT – *AND* – SHOUTED AT ME .
4.6.2 HOW I COULD'VE BOUGHT SUCH A SILLY THING – – //

4.7.1 I WAS VERY ANGRY ABOUT THIS AND SHOUTED BACK .
4.7.2 AND *SO* – WE WERE SHOUTING AT EACH OTHER THE WHOLE EVENING //

Appendix I. 4. b

NARRATIVE STRUCTURE OF EXPOSITION (Text 4)

U	SETTING	FUNCTION	TEXT
1	*General setting:* time character – action location	*General introduction:*	ONE AFTERNOON I WENT OUT SHOPPING
2	*Detailed setting:* detailed location character – action more detailed location	*Detailed introduction:* anticipation of fatal event	PASSING SEVERAL SHOPS I STOPPED AT A SHOP WHERE ANTIQUES COULD BE BOUGHT
3	*Expository event:* character – action fatal object + location fatal decision	*Introduction of theme:* "conversation piece"	I SAW A BEAUTIFUL LAMP STANDING IN THE WINDOW AND DECIDED TO BUY IT
4	explanation rationalization fatal action	retardation and arousal of tension	IT WAS QUITE EXPENSIVE BUT I LIKED IT SO MUCH AN SO I JUST BOUGHT IT
5	PLOT		AT HOME I SHOWED IT ...

Appendix I. 4. c

SCHEMA OF EXPOSITION (Text 4)

S	U	L	P	TIME	LOCATION	CHARACTER	SHOPPING
1	1	OUTSIDE THE SHOP		ONE AFTERNOON		I WENT OUT	
	2				PASSING SEVERAL SHOPS	I w[ent] / I STOPPED	on a shop / AT A SHOP — WHERE ANTIQUES COULD BE BOUGHT
	3		R			I SAW	A BEAUTIFUL LAMP STANDING IN THE pane WINDOW pane
			M	an AND		DECIDED	TO BUY IT
			R			[I went	into the shop and . . .]
	4		M	BUT / AND SO		I LIKED / I JUST BOUGHT	it wasn't [expensive] / IT WAS QUITE EXPENSIVE / IT SO MUCH / IT
2		AT HOME	R			[I went	home with it]
3	5				AT HOME	I SHOWED	IT TO MY HUSBAND . . .

REFERENCES

ADJEMIAN, C. 1976. On the Nature of Interlanguage Systems. *Language Learning.* 26, 297-320.

BARTLETT, F.C. 1932. *Remembering. A Study in Experimental and Social Psychology.* Cambridge: Cambridge University Press.

BRAINE, M.D.S. 1963. On Learning the Grammatical Order of Words. *Psychological Review.* 70, 323-348.

BRAINE, M.D.S. 1971. On Two Types of Models of the Internalization of Grammar. In: D.I. Slobin (ed.). *The Ontogenesis of Grammar. A Theoretical Symposium.* New York: Academic Press, 153-243.

BRUNER, J.S., J.J. Goodnow and G.A. Austin. 1956. *A Study of Thinking.* New York: Wiley.

CHOMSKY, N. 1959. Review of Skinner's Verbal Behavior. *Language.* 35, 26-58.

CHOMSKY, N. 1964. Current Issues in Linguistic Theory. In: J.A. Fodor and J.J. Katz (eds.). *The Structure of Language. Readings in the Philosophy of Language.* Englewood Cliffs, N.J.: Prentice Hall, 50-118.

COOPER, R.L. 1970. What Do We Learn When We Learn a Language? *TESOL Quarterly.* 4, 312-318.

CORDER, S.P. 1971. Idiosyncratic Dialects and Error Analysis. *IRAL.* 9, 147-160.

CORDER, S.P. 1974. The Elicitation of Interlanguage. *IRAL Special Issue.* Stuttgart: Groos.

CORDER, S.P. 1975a. Error Analysis, Interlanguage and Second Language Acquisition. *Language Teaching and Linguistics: Abstracts.* 8, 201-218.

CORDER, S.P. 1975b. The Language of Second Language Learners. The Broader Issue. *Modern Language Journal.* 57, 409-413.

CRYSTAL, D. and Davy, D. 1975. *Advanced Conversational English.* London: Longman.

DECHERT, H.W. forthcoming. Pauses and Intonation as Indicators of Verbal Planning in Second Language Speech Productions. In: H.W. Dechert and M. Raupach (eds.). *Temporal Variables in Speech.* The Hague: Mouton.

DEESE, J. 1978. Thought into Speech. *American Scientist.* 66, 314-321.

DICKERSON, L.J. 1975. The Learner's Interlanguage as a System of Variable Rules. *TESOL Quarterly.* 9, 401-407.

DULAY, H.C. and M.K. Burt. 1972. Goofing: an Indicator of Children's Second Language Learning Strategies. *Language Learning.* 22, 235-252.

DULAY, H.C. and M.K. Burt. 1974a. Errors and Strategies in Child Second Language Acquisition. *TESOL Quarterly.* 8, 129-136.

DULAY, H.C. and M.K. Burt. 1974b. A New Perspective on the Creative Construction Process in Child Second Language Acquisition. *Working Papers on Bilingualism.* 4, 71-98.

ERDMANN, P. 1973. Patterns of Stress-Transfer in English and German. *IRAL.* 11, 229-241.

ERVIN-TRIPP, S.M. 1973. Some Strategies for the First Two Years. In: A.S. Dil (ed.). *Language Acquisition and Communicative Choice.* Stanford: University Press, 204-238.

ERVIN-TRIPP, S.M. 1974. Is Second Language Learning Like the First? *TESOL Quarterly.* 8, 111-127.

FERGUSON, C.A. 1971. Absence of Copula and the Notion of Simplicity. In: D. Hymes (ed.). *Pidginization and Creolization of Languages.* Cambridge: Cambridge University Press, 141-150.

FERGUSON, C.A. 1975. Toward a Characterization of English Foreigner Talk. *Anthropological Linguistics.* 17, 1-14.

FROMKIN, V.A. 1971. The Non-Anomalous Nature of Anomalous Utterances. *Language.* 47, 27-52.

FROMKIN, V.A. (ed.). 1973. *Speech Errors as Linguistic Evidence.* The Hague: Mouton.

GARRETT, M.F. 1975. The Analysis of Sentence Production. In: G.H. Bower (ed.). *The Psychology of Learning and Motivation.* Vol. 9. New York: Academic Press, 133-177.

GARRETT, M.F. 1976. Syntactic Processes in Sentence Production. In: R.J. Wales and E. Walker (eds.). *New Approaches to Language Mechanisms.* Amsterdam: North-Holland, 231-256.

GOLDMAN-EISLER, F. 1961. Hesitation and Information in Speech. In: C. Cherry (ed.). *Information Theory.* London: Butterworths, 162-174.

JAMES, C. 1971. *Foreign Language Learning by Dialect Expansion.* Paper read to PAKS Symposion. Stuttgart.

JENKINS, J.J. 1977. Remember that Old Theory of Memory? Well, Forget It! In: R. Shaw and J. Bransford. *Perceiving, Acting, and Knowing.* New York: Wiley, 413-429.

KATZ, J.J. 1966. *The Philosophy of Language.* New York: Harper & Row.

KINTSCH, W. 1970. *Learning, Memory, and Conceptual Processes.* New York: Wiley.

KINTSCH, W. 1977. *Memory and Cognition.* New York: John Wiley.

KINTSCH, W. and W. Kozminsky. 1977. Summarizing Stories After Reading and Listening. *Journal of Educational Psychology.* 69, 491-499.

KRASHEN, S. 1975. *Monitor Theory.* Unpublished paper presented at the UCLA-USC Second Language Acquisition Forum.

LEVINE, M. 1975. *A Cognitive Theory of Learning. Research on Hypothesis Testing.* New York: Wiley.

MANDLER, G. 1967. Organization and Memory. In: K.W. Spence and J. Taylor Spence (eds.). *The Psychology of Learning and Motivation.* New York: Academic Press, 327-372.

MANDLER, J.M. and N.S. Johnson. 1977. Remembrance of Things Parsed: Story Structure and Recall. *Cognitive Psychology.* 9, 111-151.

McLAUGHLIN, B. 1978. *Second Language Acquisition in Childhood.* New York: Wiley.

NEMSER, W. 1971. Approximative Systems of Foreign Language Learners. *IRAL.* 9, 115-123.

PEPPER, S.C. 1948. *World Hypotheses. A Study of Evidence.* Berkeley: University of California Press.

RICHARDS, J.C. 1971a. Error Analysis and Second Language Strategies. *Language Sciences.* 4, 12-22.

RICHARDS, J.C. 1971b. A Non-Contrastive Approach to Error Analysis. *English Language Teaching.* 25, 204-219.

RICHARDS, J.C. 1972. Social Factors, Interlanguage and Language Learning. *Language Learning.* 22, 159-188.

SCHLUE, K. 1977. An Inside View of Interlanguage. In: C.A. Henning (ed.). *Proceedings of the Los Angeles Second Language Research Forum.* June 1977, 342-348.

SCHUMANN, J.H. 1974. The Implications of Interlanguage, Pidginization and Creolization for the Study of Adult Second Language Acquisition. *TESOL Quarterly.* 8, 145-152.

SCHUMANN, J.H. 1976. Implications of Pidginization and Creolization for the Study of Adult Second Language Acquisition. In: J.H. Schumann and N. Stenson (eds.). *New Frontiers in Second Language Learning.* 2nd. ed. Rowley, Mass.: Newbury House, 137-152.

SELINKER, L. 1969. Language Transfer. *General Linguistics.* 9, 67-92.

SELINKER, L. 1971. The Psychologically Relevant Data of Second-Language Learning. In: P. Pimsleur and T.A. Quinn (eds.). *The Psychology of Second Language Learning.* Cambridge: Cambridge University Press, 35-44.

SELINKER, L. 1972. Interlanguage. *IRAL.* 10, 209-231.

SELINKER, L., M. Swain and G. Dumas. 1975. The Interlanguage Hypothesis extended to Children. *Language Learning.* 25, 139-152.

SLAMA-CAZACU, T. 1971. Psycholinguistics and Contrastive Studies. *Zagreb Conference on English Contrastive Projects.* Zagreb 1971, 188-206.

TARONE, E. 1976. Some Influences on Interlanguage Phonology. *Working Papers on Bilingualism.* 8, 87-111.

TAYLOR, B.P. 1974. Toward a Theory of Language Acquisition. *Language Learning.* 24, 23-35.

TULVING, E. and Z. Pearlstone. 1966. Availability versus Accessibility of Information in Memory for Words. *Journal of Verbal Learning and Verbal Behavior.* 5, 381-391.

TEMPORAL VARIABLES IN CROSS-LINGUISTIC PSYCHOLINGUISTICS — AN ANNOTATED BIBLIOGRAPHY

Richard Wiese
University of Kassel

Introduction

Contrastive linguistics has recently adopted a new research strategy. This approach considers not only the linguistic structures of two or more languages, and the linguistic products of speakers of different languages, but also the underlying processes of planning, producing, and understanding utterances. To look for the processes taking place in bilinguals and foreign language learners is by nature a psycholinguistic undertaking. It also requires an elaborate methodology, because the phenomena studied here are neither directly observable nor even accessible through conscious introspection. The temporal characteristics of speech behaviour, which include pauses, corrections, repetitions, and hesitations, seem to provide one sort of evidence for the underlying mechanisms of speech; speech errors and slips of the tongue another. Both sources have been used extensively in the last decade to build up models of language processing.[1] Under a cross-linguistic perspective, one has to take into account several complications. The two most important are perhaps that two (or even more) language systems are (possibly) involved, and that a learner has only a limited knowledge of the language he is about to acquire. Cross-linguistic studies also involve cross-cultural considerations, as Fathman (this volume) and Samarin (1964) demonstrate.

A problem lies in the fact that there is hardly any study which does not have English as one of the languages dealt with. Though English is an important medium of communication especially as a second language, there is a deplorable lack of research into other languages. Thus conclusions about the role of different language systems and their influence on planning and production behaviour can only be speculative at the moment. The scarce evidence seems to suggest that not different language structures but different cultural rules and norms lead to different temporal characteristics of speech.

Historically, the starting point for a cross-linguistic psycho-linguistics goes back to the work of Erdmann/Dodge and Cattell, a German-American tradition, which had, in spite of remarkable results, only a short life, and which was re-

---

[1] For the study of temporal variables see Dechert and Raupach (forthcoming), for research on speech error: Fromkin (1973).

sumed again much later, sometimes without awareness of the forerunners' work. Language studies with both a cross-linguistic and a psycholinguistic approach are not very numerous, in spite of their relevance for second language learning. But there seems to be an emerging field, where the work of psycholinguists, contrastive linguists, and researchers in second language acquisition fruitfully meet. To document what has been done in this field, the following bibliography has been set up. It is but a small list; only those works are included which deal with temporal variables in speech under a psycholinguistic and cross-linguistic perspective, in a similar spirit as the contributions to this volume. This includes studies concerned with speech-production in a second or acquired language, under the assumption that L2 production is, in some way or other, influenced by L1. Within this area, the bibliography tries to be comprehensive, leaving out only shorter papers, the content of which seems to be included in other publications.

In fact, the bibliography demonstrates how litte work has been done in the field described above. Notably there is, to my knowledge, no comprehensive monograph or even survey article. Therefore the aim of this bibliography can only be to list the scattered papers and articles to provide a starting point for further more systematic and intensive studies. The abstracts given under each title necessarily leave out many aspects of the articles. They concentrate, according to the problem space outlined above, on the results found in studies on temporal variables in contrastive psycholinguistics.

The work done so far opens more questions than it answers. A few which appear from the literature might be listed here:

— What kind of methodology is necessary, so that temporal variables can be used as indicators for planning processes without destroying conditions for a natural flow of speech?

— Are pauses a part of the language structure, should they be integrated into a grammar? The differences between languages found so far are small but partly significant. If languages show distinct pause structures, one has to conclude that the temporal organization is part of the linguistic structure of a language, and not only a feature of speech behaviour.

— How deep-going are the differences between first and second language productions?

— Should or can the temporal organization of a language be taught in foreign language classes?

Bibliography

BARIK, H.C. 1973. Simultaneous Interpretation: Temporal and Quantitative Data. *Language and Speech.* 16, 237-270.

English-dominant and French-dominant interpreters (professionals, students, and amateurs) interpreted simultaneously texts from different speech-genres and both from English and from French. The temporal characteristics of speakers of the original texts and of the interpreters were analysed and compared. "... the translator tries to take advantage of the speaker's pauses and thereby reduces the extent of time during which he must be both speaking and listening at the same time. Characteristically, the translator lags behind the speaker in his delivery by 2 to 3 sec. The temporal data do not in general reveal striking differences in relation to the different categories of the translator, the various types of material, or the two directions of translation."

BEARDSLEY, R.B. and C.M. Eastman. 1971. Markers, Pauses and Code Switching in Bilingual Tanzanian Speech. *General Linguistics.* 11, 17-27.

A study of code-switching between English and Swahili shows that code-switching is often associated with markers (particles without semantic content or syntactic function) and pauses. Both markers and pauses may be good indicators of a switch and reflect difficulties in utterance planning.

BELLUGI, U. and S. Fischer. 1972. A Comparison of Sign Language and Spoken Language: Rate and Grammatical Mechanisms. *Cognition.* 1, 173-200.

A study of the temporal organization of languages in different modalities: The American Sign Language (ASL) and English. Subjects bilingual in English and ASL were asked to tell a story in ASL, English, and in both languages simultaneously. "The rate of articulation for speaking is considerably higher than the rate of articulation for signing, even when both languages are produced at the same time." (p. 183) Nevertheless the time needed for expressing a proposition was nearly the same in the different modalities. The modality specific features of ASL allow for time saving mechanisms, though it takes more time to produce a sign than a spoken word.

CATTELL, J. 1885. Ueber die Zeit der Erkennung von Schriftzeichen, Bildern und Farben. *Philosophische Studien.* 2, 635-650.

The reading rate of English and German speaking subjects was measured with a chronometer, using English, German, French, Italian, Latin, and Greek texts. The rate of reading letters and words varied mainly with the knowledge of the respective language, but depended also on whether letters or words were part of a meaningful string (words, sentences).

CATTELL, J. 1886. The Time It Takes to See and Name Objects. *Mind.* 11, 63-65.

Summary of Cattell (1885).

DECHERT, H.W. forthcoming. Pauses and Intonation as Indicators of Verbal Planning in Second-Language Speech Productions: Two Examples from a Case Study. In: H.W. Dechert and M. Raupach (eds.). *Temporal Variables in Speech*. The Hague: Mouton.

A case study with a German student of English, who retold a story (Bartlett's 'The War of the Ghosts') twice, before and after a visit to the U.S.A. The second, more fluent version shows that he has improved his ability to solve lower level speech planning problems. Intonation contours and pauses in the productions mark a particular kind of speech unit, called 'episodic unit', because it corresponds to units in the story structure.

ERDMANN, B. and R. Dodge. 1898. *Psychologische Untersuchungen über das Lesen auf experimenteller Grundlage*. Halle: Niemeyer.

On the basis of the German psychophysiological theory of the 19th century, Erdmann/Dodge study the processes involved in recognition of letters and words. Eye movements and time length for perceptual processes are taken as data for a theory of reading. Meaningful letter sequences (words and sentences) need a shorter recognition time than chance combinations: the important factor is the subject's familiarity with the letter string. The results include data for both English and German as foreign and native languages: Native words are easier to recognize than foreign. Reading is not so much the successive perception of letters but rather the simultaneous apperception of greater units.

ERVIN-TRIPP, S. 1970. An Analysis of the Interaction of Language, Topic and Listener. In: J.A. Fishman (ed.). *Readings in the Sociology of Language*. The Hague, Paris: Mouton. 192-211.

Bilingual Japanese-American women were interviewed in English or Japanese on an American or Japanese topic. When interviewed in English (by a Japanese) on a Japanese topic, "they borrowed more Japanese words, had more disturbed syntax, were less fluent, and had more frequent hesitation pauses." (p. 205)

GOLDMAN-EISLER, F. 1972. Segmentation of Input in Simultaneous Translation. *Journal of Psycholinguistic Research*. 1, 127-140.

This paper examines the monitoring behaviour of simultaneous translators. Records of simultaneous translations from English to French, French to English, and German to English are analyzed with respect to the length and the nature of the segments the interpreter needs to decode and encode speech. The unit of monitoring very often corresponds to a proposition. Due to the final position of the verb in many German sentences, the chunks to be stored before translation are often longer than in English or French. The simultaneity of the different cognitive processes is discussed as well.

GOLDMAN-EISLER, F. and M. Cohen. 1975. An Experimental Study of Interference between Receptive and Productive Processes Relating to Simultaneous Translation. *Linguistics*. 151, 5-16.

"The question of the interference between the reception and production of speech is basic to an understanding of the processes involved in simultaneous translation. This paper reports an experiment designed to throw light on this problem by controlling the level of interference between decoding and encoding speech using hesitancy as an indicator of interference. This proved effective in spotting the levels at which interference takes place. Encoding without processing did not interfere with the monitoring of even highly complex intellectual material, but encoding involving complex processing did so in proportion to the hesitancy of the input. Such encoding was facilitated at the end of monitored sentences and inhibited while they were being monitored." (Abstract, p. 15)

GROSJEAN, F. forthcoming. *Comparative Studies of Temporal Variables in Spoken and Sign Languages: A Short Review.* In: H.W. Dechert and M. Raupach (eds.). *Temporal Variables in Speech.* The Hague: Mouton.

American Sign Language (ASL) as a visual language is compared in its temporal patterning to spoken language (English). The pause structures differ for visual and spoken languages, though the amount of information per time unit is the same. Pausing in speech and in signing is of a different character (breathing vs. hands in rest position), whereas the relation of pauses to structural and utterance boundaries appears to be the same across modality differences.

HAGGAN, M. 1973. *Cross-Linguistic Aspects of Pausing.* Unpublished Ph. D. Thesis, University College London.

A series of experiments on the temporal characteristics of native Arabic and English speakers and Arabic learners of English. Hesitation phenomena and comprehension of native speakers vs. learners and the relation of pausing to semantic planning are also discussed.

KOWAL, S., D.C. O'Connell, E. O'Brien, and E.T. Bryant. 1975. Temporal Aspects of Reading Aloud and Speaking: Three Experiments. *American Journal of Psychology.* 88, 549-569.

"Three different experiments on the effects of linguistic development or proficiency on temporal aspects of reading aloud and speaking assessed the frequency, length, and location of unfilled pauses, speech rate, and phrase length. In general, proficiency decreased the frequency and length of those pauses and increased speech rate and phrase length when the subjects were reading, whereas it only increased speech rate and phrase length, and produced a sensitivity to semantic variations, when they were retelling a story. These findings, the exceptions to them, and the effect of the specific location of the pauses on their length suggest a pretheoretical distinction between the pauses' linguistic and cognitive functions." (Abstract, p. 549)

LANE, H., F. Grosjean, J. Le Berre, and E. Lewin. 1973. Exploring Some Properties of Foreign-Language Utterances that Control Their Comprehension. *Linguistics*. 112, 15-22.

Temporal variables, syntactic complexity, and textual coherence (thematic shift) are studied as factors which control text comprehension by second language learners. In an experiment with French students of English, the increase in comprehension was measured for high and low values for these properties. Number of pauses, articulation rate, and textual coherence ('rhetorical entropy') was found to have significant results, but syntactic complexity appeared to be the most powerful factor.

MEARA, P. forthcoming. Probe Latencies, Foreign Languages and Foreign Language Learners. In: H.W. Dechert and M. Raupach (eds.). *Temporal Variables in Speech*. The Hague: Mouton.

Native speakers and learners of Spanish undertook a probe latency test with Spanish sentences. Contrary to all assumptions, the reaction time corresponded to the importance of constituent boundaries only in the case of learners, not of native speakers. It is proposed that because of the syntactic structure of Spanish the NP / VP boundary does not have the prominent psychological reality it has in English.

O'CONNELL, D.C. and S. Kowal. 1972. Cross-Linguistic Pause and Rate Phenomena in Adults and Adolescents. *Journal of Psycholinguistic Research*. 1, 155-164.

German and American subjects, adults and adolescents, read and retold two stories. The amount of pausing increased with semantically deviant or unusual material in the stories. Thus the cognitive function of pauses seems to be established, without excluding other possible sources of pausing.

OSSER, H. and F. Peng. 1964. A Cross-Cultural Study of Speech Rate. *Language and Speech*. 7, 120-125.

"This paper describes an experimental attempt to investigate the 'cultural stereotype' judgment of speech-rate, i.e. the judgment that people speaking in a language that is foreign to the listener always appear to be talking very rapidly. Two samples of speech were obtained from 6 native Japanese speakers and 6 native American-English speakers. Analyses of both samples failed to reveal significant differences in speech-rate between the two groups. Some implications of the results are formulated and finally several hypotheses are proposed to account for the 'cultural stereotype' judgment of speech-rate." (Abstract, p. 120)

PÜRSCHEL, H. 1975. *Pause und Kadenz. Interferenzerscheinungen bei der englischen Intonation deutscher Sprecher*. Tübingen: Niemeyer.

After reviewing the literature on interference, intonation, and pauses, the author describes an experiment where German students of English are asked to read an

English text and a comparable German version. Pause distributions and intonation contours are compared on the basis of the assumption that interference takes place also in the prosodic area. The results show more pauses in the English readings, less interference with students who have been more exposed to native speakers, and a tendency to segment the text according to the rules of the first language.

RAMSAY, R.W. 1968. Speech Patterns and Personality. *Language and Speech*. 11, 54-63.

A study about the interaction of personality variables (extraversion, introversion, sex, etc.) with pausal phenomena. Compared to the results of Goldman-Eisler, Dutch subjects in this study showed patterns in pauses and hesitations comparable to English speakers.

RAUPACH, M. forthcoming. Temporal Variables in First and Second Language Speech Production. In: H.W. Dechert and M. Raupach (eds.). *Temporal Variables in Speech*. The Hague: Mouton.

French and German students gave cartoon descriptions, both in their native language and in German and French as their respective second language. The results showed (1) differences in pauses and hesitations between the French and the German native language productions, (2) differing pausal structures in the L2 productions (more pauses, slower articulation rates). The latter are attributed to the learner's abilities in the second language and to the nature of the task.(3) A case study of one French and one German subject reveals a tendency to transfer temporal characteristics from the L1 into the L2 productions: greater or less fluency in a second language is partly a function of fluency in the first language.

SAMARIN, W. 1964. Language of Silence. *Practical Anthropology*. 11, 115-119.

Silence, the pausing between speechsounds, can have a meaning of its own. This meaning varies cross-culturally as shown by the author's experience with a Central African tribe.